FIRM
FEEDBACK
IN A
FRAGILE
WORLD

FIRM FEEDBACK
IN A
FRAGILE WORLD

HOW TO **BUILD A WINNING CULTURE** WITH **CRITICAL CONVERSATIONS**

BY JEFF HANCHER

Firm Feedback in a Fragile World: How to Build a Winning Culture with Critical Conversations
Copyright © 2025 by Jeff Hancher

All rights reserved. No part of this publication may be reproduced, stored in a retrieval system, or transmitted in any form by any means, electronic, mechanical, photocopy, recording, or otherwise, without the prior permission of the publisher, except as provided by USA copyright law.

No patent liability is assumed with respect to the use of the information contained herein. Although every precaution has been taken in the preparation of this book, the publisher and author assume no responsibility for errors or omissions. Neither is any liability assumed for damages resulting from the use of the information contained herein.

Some names and identifying details have been changed to protect the privacy of individuals.

Published by Maxwell Leadership Publishing, an imprint of Forefront Books.
Distributed by Simon & Schuster.

Library of Congress Control Number: 2025902723

Print ISBN: 979-8-88710-047-0
E-book ISBN: 979-8-88710-048-7

Cover Design by George Stevens, G Sharp Design
Interior Design by PerfecType, Nashville, TN

Printed in the United States of America

To my wife, Janelle,

Your unwavering love, encouragement, and belief in me have been foundational in everything I do. This book exists because of your steadfast support and the sacrifices you have made to help me pursue my calling. You are my greatest blessing, my partner, my inspiration, and my best friend. Thank you for walking this journey with me—I dedicate this work and all that I am to you.

CONTENTS

Foreword **9**

A Note from Mark Cole **13**

Introduction: Our Fragile World **17**

CHAPTER 1 The Transformational Power of Feedback **33**

CHAPTER 2 Your Feedback Inheritance **45**

CHAPTER 3 Relationships Build a Foundation for Feedback **61**

CHAPTER 4 Earning the Right to Hold Others Accountable **79**

CHAPTER 5 Clarifying Misunderstandings About Feedback **95**

CHAPTER 6 FEAR: The Four Reasons Most People Avoid Giving Feedback **105**

CHAPTER 7 Directive Feedback: When Clarity Counts **125**

CONTENTS

CHAPTER 8 Collaborative Feedback: Building Bridges, Not Walls   137

CHAPTER 9 Supportive Feedback: Building Confidence Through Encouragement   157

CHAPTER 10 Providing Accountability: The Backbone of Leadership   175

CHAPTER 11 Eliminating Blind Spots: How Leaders Can Grow Their Feedback Skills   197

CHAPTER 12 Building Your Leadership Legacy: Making Feedback Your Gift to Others   213

Acknowledgments   **227**

Notes   **229**

FOREWORD

By Tim Elmore

I believe there are few topics more important to address in the workplace than this one. How do you muster courage from within to host that tough conversation? What must you do to stop avoiding that poor performing teammate, host a conversation, and develop a game plan for him or her to improve? It's the part of leadership that most executives hate the most.

Why is this true?

I believe it's because to provide tough feedback to an employee, and to do it well, requires emotional security. That's something you don't learn in an MBA class. It is certainly not for the faint of heart. It requires backbone. And even with some backbone, it's still not easy or fun. It's the kind of thing that keeps you up at night, wondering how your team member will react. Will it cause them to withdraw? Will you never enjoy the same relationship again? Then you begin to question if you even

FOREWORD

have the time for this long, emotional conversation? Will it demotivate everyone in the department? And what if you're wrong about the issue? Would it be better just to leave the issue alone?

On top of all that is the day in which we live.

According to some experts, particularly when discussing younger generations like Millennials and Generation Z, there is a growing concern that society may be raising a "fragile generation" due to increased overprotection, heightened focus on safety, and a culture of avoiding discomfort, leaving individuals ill-equipped to handle challenges and setbacks in life. This is certainly not true of every young professional, but more than half of today's working population grew up in a "cancel culture." By this I mean society has conditioned people to think that the answer to hardship is to remove it. In fact, why not cancel anything that makes us uncomfortable? I have a friend who served seven years in the Navy. When I asked how he enjoyed serving, he replied, "Well, it was different than I thought it would be." I inquired what he meant by his remark, and he said with a straight face, "Our drill sergeant gave us all a card to hold up in the air if he said anything that made us feel uncomfortable."

I don't mean to oversimplify the complex time we live in. There are lots we don't know about the struggles people endure. But I do know one thing: Good leadership will always require difficult decisions and tough conversations. Peter Drucker once said, "Whenever you see a successful organization, somebody at some time made a courageous decision."

One of my Habitudes® illustrates what Jeff Hancher speaks of here. It's called, "The Velvet Covered Brick." That's how leaders offer feedback: velvet on the outside (grace, warmth, and belief), brick on the inside (candor, principled, and truthful). Consider this: We are working in an era that is more polarized and avoidant than any period in my forty-five-year career. We must get this right. I began my career working for John C. Maxwell, serving under his leadership for twenty years, before launching my own organization. When I'm asked what's the top leadership lesson I learned under Dr. Maxwell, I never hesitate in my answer. It was this topic: How do I enter a challenging conversation, provide firm feedback, and even confront a situation that needs attention.

This book by my friend Jeff Hancher contains the insights you'll need to do this well. He has practiced what he preaches in this volume for years, and he possesses the wisdom to walk you through the process. This book simplifies a complicated topic and furnishes step-by-step counsel for any leader who faces a teammate who needs your help but may be unaware or too afraid to ask. When someone on your team needs you to say, "Can we talk?" I suggest you digest this volume, then take the plunge and host that conversation. Now you'll know how.

FOREWORD

Thank you, Jeff, for putting this wisdom into print. We are grateful.

Tim Elmore
Founder
TimElmore.com
GrowingLeaders.com

A NOTE FROM MARK COLE

Have you ever heard someone else's idea and thought, "I wish I thought of that myself?" That's how I feel about this book.

I met Jeff Hancher in January 2024, where he had the opportunity to pitch his idea for the book you are now holding in your hands. Jeff talked about how the power of feedback could change people's lives and, ultimately, give them a better future. His book would teach leaders how to give meaningful feedback while also creating solid relationships between the leader and their employees.

I was captivated by his content, but more than that, I was impressed by how he captured the attention of everyone in that room. His passion for what he wanted to share with the world was contagious.

I've been in the leadership development business for decades, and I genuinely believe that giving firm feedback is an area where many leaders struggle. Fear over losing people or even developing a bad reputation (among countless other insecurities) stops leaders from giving the constructive criticism their employees need.

As I shared this with Jeff, it hit me! "Firm Feedback in a Fragile World," I said. "That's the title of your book. That's what you're teaching people." Leaders can learn techniques for communicating to people and scripts for phrasing their feedback. But there's so much more that's required to give teams the feedback they need.

What you find in leadership is that the strongest leaders are the ones who have earned the right to lead well through relational integrity. They have both technical and emotional intelligence. So not only will you get better at giving feedback by reading this book, you will also gain the tools needed to become a leader people *want* to follow—not just a leader people *have* to follow.

This book will teach you that feedback doesn't need to create tension between you and your employees. It can be used as a tool to help employees achieve the career and the life they have always wanted. That's what great leaders do after all. They don't lead for their own success; they lead for the success of others. Leaders who embrace this stop living a life of success and start living a life of significance.

As the CEO of Maxwell Leadership, I've had the opportunity to travel the world and help develop leaders from many cultures. I often find leaders are intimidated to be assertive and give clear feedback for fear of a

A NOTE FROM MARK COLE

feedback recoil. But this book solves one of the most universal leadership challenges that I see around the world. Here is my encouragement to you as you read this book: Enjoy the ride as Jeff helps you overcome the challenge of delivering firm feedback and equips and empowers you to reach your full leadership potential.

Mark Cole
CEO of Maxwell Leadership Enterprises

INTRODUCTION
Our Fragile World

No one smiled or engaged in polite small talk while we shuffled into the conference room. As we took our seats around the large wooden table, some frantically flipped through notes, while others clutched their coffee cups, looking like they hadn't slept.

Here we go again, I thought.

That Sunday evening, our boss, Matt, had sent an email to the entire sales team, summoning us to this meeting. The message had said we "needed to talk." But we knew Matt would be the one doing the talking.

What a way to start a Monday—filled with dread.

Even so, I didn't blame him for wanting to address our team's recent decline in sales. Our usually successful division was starting to miss our monthly targets.

Matt entered the room and wasted no time going over pages of data reinforcing that our results were unacceptable. As he shared this feedback, his volume rarely fell below shouting.

When he was finished, he sighed and said, "Who thinks they know how we can fix this?"

The room was quiet except for the sound of a few people shuffling the papers in front of them. So Jon, one of our other sales leaders, spoke up. "I think I know why we're struggling," he said. He went on to explain where in the sales process he thought the problem was. Then he presented a strategy that had worked well for him in the past that he thought we could modify to meet our current needs.

Matt leaned onto the table and practically yelled, "And that's why your results *suck*, Jon!"

The room was silent for a moment as everyone else looked down at their cups or reinspected their notes so they could avoid eye contact with Matt or Jon.

"We can't keep doing the same crap and expect better results. Does anyone have a better idea?"

. Unsurprisingly, no one did. In fact, no one said a word for the rest of the meeting. The way this leader responded to Jon's suggestions completely derailed the conversation and prevented the team from collaborating on a possible solution.

Matt's reaction is just one of the many extreme ways I have seen leaders and employees alike respond to feedback.

INTRODUCTION

To put it simply, feedback is the process where information (data) is given and received with the intent of modifying or reinforcing the next action. Matt had received feedback from his boss in the form of our team's sales trends. During our meeting with Matt, he received feedback from Jon on the potential cause of that decrease. If feedback is just data, why did Matt become so upset?

Anger isn't the only reaction people can have to feedback. When I worked in a corporate office, I had an excellent administrative assistant. I loved working with her. She understood my strengths and weaknesses and made my job easier. When we sat down for one of our usual one-on-one meetings, Karen was suddenly quiet. She avoided making eye contact with me. I started to wonder if something was seriously wrong with Karen or her family. I immediately exited business mode and prepared to give her my utmost support.

"Karen, are you okay?" I asked. "What's going on?"

Tears fell from her eyes and wet the desk in front of her. "I just don't feel like anything I do is ever good enough for you."

For a moment, I felt frozen, watching her cry. Somewhere along the line, Karen had started responding negatively to my feedback. Now, it looked like my relationship with one of my best employees was in jeopardy. I felt shell-shocked because I had thought things were going really well. My company was going through a lot of change at the time, and I didn't know how I would function if she decided to quit. I knew I had to continue to give her feedback, but how could I if every time I did, I risked her responding like this?

You've probably asked yourself similar questions when counting the cost of giving feedback. "How will they respond?" "Is it even necessary to give this feedback?" "What if they disagree?" "How is this going to affect our relationship?"

In my time as a leader, I've experienced many unique responses to feedback. I wish I could tell you that these stories are the exception, not the rule, but feedback often creates an emotional—and in some cases bizarre—response.

Just hearing the words "We need to talk" can put some people on the defensive right away. Even the thought of receiving bad news or unwanted feedback makes their heart beat a little bit faster and their defenses rise.

According to a 2017 study by Paul Green,[1] people tend to move away from negative feedback. So, when employees are corrected or shown how they could improve, they tend to move away from the person who gave them the feedback. The more people give negative feedback, the more people isolate themselves. I've heard from leaders who have experienced everything from

INTRODUCTION

employees giving them the silent treatment to simply not returning to work. These leaders were left with fractured communication, workplace tension, and, at times, an empty position on their team.

You probably have your own stories of how people have responded to feedback. Maybe you've had an employee curse at you after you gave them unwanted feedback, or you've been on the receiving end of a bad performance review when you thought you were doing well. You may not have quit or burst into tears, but you probably experienced a negative emotional response. Were you worried you would be fired? Were you upset that you were being blamed for someone else's mistake? Were you offended that your boss was micromanaging your work?

Feedback often produces emotional responses, which leads to leaders feeling insecure about offering feedback. Our worlds feel so fragile, both at work and at home, that the risk of giving feedback seems to outweigh the benefits. In fact, nearly seven out of ten managers report feeling uncomfortable delivering feedback to their employees.[2] And despite the managers' responses, 75 percent of employees say they need *more* feedback! Our fears and lack of skills surrounding feedback have created a workplace and a culture that is starved for feedback.

Why Employees Struggle to Accept Feedback

One of the biggest culprits of absent or ineffective feedback is poor communication skills. Without solid communication skills, leaders struggle to express what they need and provide clear direction to their employees. This gap in skills can be attributed to a lack of training in how to communicate, along with generational and cultural differences.

Consider that you can have up to five generations in your workplace at any given time, from the Silent Generation and baby boomers to Gen Xers, millennials, and Gen Zers. Each generation has its own history, culture, and life experiences that dictate the way they communicate and their attitudes toward work. Older generations can mistakenly label younger generations as lazy because they have different priorities and express them differently. At the same time, younger generations accuse older generations of being workaholics and resistant to change. Add to that different communication styles, economic backgrounds, and sociopolitical landscapes, and it can be hard to know how to talk to a member of a different generation, much less lead them.

When giving feedback to one another, different generations make assumptions about people based on their age or background and let it affect the way they give feedback. Older leaders may be harder on younger

INTRODUCTION

leaders because the latter do not have what their elders perceive as the same work ethic. Younger generations leading older employees may find themselves frustrated by the latter's attitude toward work or preference to use outdated methods. Even unconscious biases and misunderstandings have the potential to derail a feedback conversation and create unwanted conflict.

Misunderstandings like these can be amplified by the many mediums people use to communicate online. Every person has a unique style of written communication, with some preferring grammatically precise writing while others take a more relaxed, emoji-heavy approach. Different punctuation means different things to different people. You could write the same message to three people, and they could take it in three entirely different ways! This lack of continuity can create opportunities for miscommunication, hurt feelings, and decreased productivity. Leaders who want to make their employees feel valued must navigate more potential land mines than ever before.

In a world where how you feel at work is becoming increasingly valued, leaders are trying to understand how to give feedback in a way their team can accept. However, all you have to do is look on social media to know that having an open discourse is more complex than ever. How often have you read the comments under a controversial post to see strangers arguing about who is right without genuinely listening to the arguments the other side is making?

While this discourse happens often online, it happens less often offline as people struggle to find ways to express themselves and speak to others with different opinions. Because of decreased discourse and the dehumanization of those different from us, it becomes harder and harder to find safe spaces to have tough conversations. The more divided our world becomes, the more difficult it is to create the level of safety necessary to find common ground.

While it might be tempting to attribute our cultural reaction to feedback to social movements or the perceived safety of digital discourse, emotional responses are a universally adapted evolutionary response to a perceived threat. Your brain is wired to fight or flee when dealing with something that could threaten you. You may not be fighting a bear in the woods or trying to hunt a meal for your family, but biologically, receiving feedback that threatens your sense of safety and your ability to provide for those you care about feels the same. As long as you continue to feel unsafe, your brain will do what is necessary to create feelings of safety and control. That is why feedback will not be successful in an environment where your employees do not feel safe.

Feelings of safety are also impacted by cultural and economic components. Beginning in the 1970s, we saw

INTRODUCTION

a generation of people who were sick of fighting endless wars and feeling the stress of the constant threat of mutually assured destruction. Throughout the first part of the twenty-first century, employees have faced numerous economic experiences, from the Great Recession to the challenges of inflation after the peak of the COVID-19 pandemic. Culturally, attitudes toward work have shifted, and employees are exercising more of their preferences regarding where and how they work. Companies are trying to navigate those needs and desires while also meeting their business objectives. The more tension between the needs of companies and the needs and desires of their employees, the more distrust is created.

Social media has also caused people to become suspicious of what they see. It's easy to lie on social media and project a life that is far different from the reality you live. Younger generations who grew up seeing picture-perfect posting grids and even strategic vulnerability are easily put off by leaders who appear to be fake. They are looking for someone they can trust. They want to connect with people in a genuine way, but they have high standards.

They have also seen many leaders' reputations destroyed on social media. Sometimes, those leaders were exposed after committing a crime or covering up injustice in their organization. Other times, comments from their past were used against their present efforts. When leaders do not live up to their employees' standards, it can cause a crisis of trust. Anti-work and anti-career attitudes encourage people to approach their leaders with skepticism. Leaders who lose their employees' trust will quickly see increased disengagement, rising conflict, and a loss of influence.

Why Leaders Struggle to Give Feedback

No matter how big or small your leadership role is, leaders must manage people who are making decisions based on their own family needs, career goals, and emotional health. At the same time, leaders are trying to navigate their own needs in those same areas. You might be dealing with a frightening medical diagnosis while trying to manage an employee who is about to have their first child. Or maybe you were just passed up for a promotion, and you are also leading someone who is at risk of being fired if they don't change something soon. This balancing act leaves many leaders feeling tired, frustrated, and unsure of how to proceed.

Additionally, leaders are challenged with how to lead disengaged employees. Colloquially known as *quiet quitting*, this involves employees doing just enough work to avoid being fired. That's not to say every employee who desires to stick to tasks in their job description while enforcing boundaries with their time is quiet quitting. Disengaged employees are also disinterested in their work and the mission around it. They are not looking for ways to benefit the company, and they do not feel that the company is doing anything to benefit them personally or professionally. They're just waiting (or actively looking) for a different job opportunity.

While these employees remain in your organization, they are causing decreased productivity and placing additional stress on other employees. Quiet quitting costs businesses a combined $9 trillion each year in lost productivity, replacement costs, and inefficiency.[3] When disengaged employees do leave, they cost even more money and time in lost productivity. Leaders who notice disengaged employees must find ways to reengage them.

Faced with the conflict between protecting their own jobs and losing employees if they push too hard, many leaders struggle to know how to respond. The pressure to get results will cause some leaders to overcompensate. Some feel that if they don't come out strong against failure, they will be walked all over. They don't want to mess up their first leadership role or get called into their boss's office because their team is underperforming. So, they micromanage everyone. Nothing is ever good enough for them, and they will make sure you fully understand that anything less than perfection is unacceptable.

Other leaders take the opposite approach. They resist giving feedback, even when their employees are creating more work for them because they don't want to hurt anyone's feelings. They're afraid of creating a bad reputation or being "told on." They think that if they just work hard enough, they can make up for other people's mistakes, and then everything will be fine.

I've landed on both sides of this spectrum at different points in my career. As a young leader, I was told that it was better to be strict and loosen up later rather than having to tighten up later, so I came out of the gate too strong. However, after seeing one of my employees retaliate against me over feedback they didn't like, I drifted to the other side of the spectrum, afraid of upsetting another employee and losing my job.

Giving feedback can cause leaders to feel like they are walking a tightrope. If they move too far in one direction, they risk upsetting their employees and creating turnover. If they move too far in the other direction, they risk creating an unmanageable volume of work for themselves or lowering their standards. The risks of avoiding feedback are high, but the risks of giving bad feedback are even higher. In a world where we are looking for ways to find stability and comfort, feedback feels like it has the potential to create instability and tension.

INTRODUCTION

The Problem and the Missing Piece

Leaders must answer the question, How can I create a space where people feel safe enough to receive feedback? Companies are looking for creative ways to solve this problem by engaging their employees and creating a fun, collaborative environment. You may have noticed companies struggling to find the right balance between working from home and working in the office. In one sense they want to understand what kind of reward structure makes people the most productive, and in another they're trying to manufacture a culture so that their teams are kind and helpful toward each other.

Leaders who are searching for the missing piece to success by adding pizza parties or a home-office budget are looking in the wrong places. The most effective way to overcome quiet quitting and anti-career attitudes is by giving consistent, meaningful feedback.

> *The most effective way to overcome quiet quitting and anti-career attitudes is by giving consistent, meaningful feedback.*

So why aren't companies focused on training their leaders on how to give meaningful feedback?

In part, it's because leaders don't recognize that it is a problem. Gallup found that 65 percent of managers believe that they are giving meaningful feedback,[4] but a separate study of millennials in the workplace shows that only 17 percent of employees agree.[5] The lack of meaningful feedback is contributing to record-high levels of disengagement. Learning the skills necessary to deliver feedback, regardless of what is going on personally or professionally, is the first step to creating a healthy, productive culture.

Whenever I am invited to train leaders on how to manage employee performance, many of them share that this is the first real training they are getting on how to give feedback. No one is teaching this crucial skill. Instead of having a healthy team where everyone is able to give and receive feedback, leaders struggle to know how to hold people accountable. Managers tiptoe around some employees and pile work on others to try to make up the difference. At best, they are leading unhealthy teams that are not living up to their potential. At worst, some of the leaders I talk to are unable to reach their goals and are contemplating either leaving their position or, if they are owners, shutting the doors of their business for good.

Those I work with often become emotional thinking about how their team and even their company can be different if they apply what they learned to their organization. After one workshop, an executive named Linda walked up to me and tearfully said, "I can't believe no one has taught me this before." She explained that she

INTRODUCTION

had been in leadership for decades but never understood how she could support her team while holding them to high standards. "This is going to change the way I lead for good," she said. "I can't wait to get back to work and start implementing these strategies with my team."

Her excitement wasn't just because she had a strategy that had been missing up to this point in her leadership career. She was excited because she saw a way to deal with the delicate situations she found herself in as a leader, a way that would serve both her company and her employees.

If you want to create a strong foundation for your team, you must start with creating a culture that understands and embraces feedback. Much of the tension in today's workplace occurs when bosses feel that employees are operating only in their self-interest and employees feel that their boss is operating in their own self-interest. Employees don't want feedback on how they can make the CEO more money or get their boss another promotion. They want feedback that is connected to *their* personal and professional goals. Healthy organizations create an environment where people can thrive and learn the skills they need to meet their own definition of success.

I can confidently say that I wouldn't be where I am today without feedback. My life was changed dramatically because I was connected to leaders who took the time to care not just about my work but about me.

Doesn't that sound great? Wouldn't you like to work for a company where you can support your employees in their personal and professional goals while generating quality work for your company? If so, the question becomes this: Are you willing to do what it takes?

Reflection Questions

How have you observed feedback as a problem in your work culture?

Do you think you have a healthy approach to giving and receiving feedback?

Application Activity

This week make a note each time you give or receive feedback at work. At the end of the week reflect on these exchanges: How were they handled? What emotions arose out of each interaction? Did they result in positive outcomes? Did you avoid them? Why or why not?

CHAPTER 1

The Transformational Power of Feedback

Of all the factors that contribute to how people respond to feedback, a crisis at home can be one of the most devastating for the employee and the most challenging for the leader.

From a young age, most teachers and authority figures had a hard time knowing how to deal with me because of the extreme family situation I was in. Statistically, I should probably be either incarcerated or dead by now. My brother and I grew up in poverty. Both of my parents spent their adult lives on government assistance due to physical disabilities. My mother suffered from lupus, and my dad suffered from severe osteoarthritis. Neither one held a job because they were often in and out of the hospital.

We frequently went to the drugstore to get my mom's prescriptions, sometimes several times in the same week. When we arrived back home, my mom cut every pill in half, hoping to extend the amount of time between refills and avoid additional copays we could not afford.

As I grew older and became more aware of our situation, I became motivated to earn money to help the family. As early as ninth grade, I started spending my free time working odd jobs so I could keep myself clothed and fed. I used any means necessary to make money and, at one point, had a thriving resale business.

It may not have been a wonderful childhood, but I loved my parents and hated seeing them try to make do with so little. I knew I wanted to give them a better life, but I had no direction and no one to show me how to be a functional adult. I spent some time in the United States Army, had a few brushes with the law, and finally realized that if I wanted to be successful, I had to stop messing around. I applied to college and was set to start in the fall.

Just before the semester started, I got a call from my dad. Mom was being put back on hospice care, and he wouldn't be able to take care of her because he was having his foot amputated that same week. When given the choice to go to school or care for my family, I chose family. I withdrew from college and began looking for a career that could capitalize on the one skill I knew I had: hard work. After trying a few jobs, I finally found a position as a service truck driver that offered benefits and the promise of a promotion.

I started to work my way up in the company. They let drivers make upsells; if you made upsells, you got a commission. I quickly realized I liked the rush of making a sale and liked the commissions even more. Getting into sales was my big break.

Until just five months into starting my first full-time sales job, when my mom died at just forty-seven years old.

I was devastated.

I had been told for years that she would die soon. I couldn't tell you how many times she was put on hospice care and would then recover. I think I was in shock that it actually happened. She was really gone. I wouldn't be taking her to any more doctor's appointments or sitting in any more family rooms waiting for a doctor to brief me on the latest developments. She was gone.

Part of me was relieved that she wasn't in pain anymore, but a large part of me was lost. Without my mom to provide for, I felt like my motivation was gone. I was grieving the loss of my mother and, in a way, the loss of a piece of my purpose and identity.

I still showed up to work every day, but I had a hard time capturing the motivation I had when I'd started just a few months earlier. Every rejection further fueled my belief that this job wasn't worth it. Surely, it wouldn't be long until my boss would write me up because I wasn't hitting my sales targets. But what else would I do?

I walked into work just a few weeks after Mom died, thinking about all of these things. How would I provide for my family if I couldn't get back on track? Did I need to get a new job? What if I had to go back to manual labor? Could my body even handle that anymore? My world was falling apart, and I didn't know how to fix it. As I arrived at my desk, I saw a message that my boss wanted me to meet him in his office.

I had met Sean in his office before. As a new employee, I met with him to discuss my goals and how he could support me in achieving them. We also met to review some of my mistakes in the sales process. Sean offered to coach me and role-play some situations so I could close more sales. But I wondered how different this time would be. What would he have to say? And would this meeting just be the beginning of me losing my job?

Before I get into exactly what Sean said, I want you to think about the three leaders who have made the greatest impact on your life.

You may be thinking of a coach, teacher, mentor, parent, or pastor. I ask this question at every leadership workshop I facilitate, and I'll never forget the stories I have heard. Like Dan, who told me about the youth pastor who challenged him to act like the man he wanted to become. Or Evan's college basketball coach, who helped him to overcome the negative mindsets that prevented him from pushing himself in practice. Or Sharon, whose boss took her under her wing and supported her after she moved across the country and away from her family to take on a new job. Regardless of the situation, the people asked agreed that without these leaders, they would never have had the skills, confidence, or fortitude to get where they are today.

What about you? Have you identified your three?

Now answer this question: Were they tough on you?

I'm sure you're nodding your head *yes*. Dan sure was: His youth pastor "pushed me harder than anyone and wasn't afraid to call me out when I needed it." To truly make an impact, leaders must take action to help you make positive changes in the way you approach your life, career, and personal goals.

> *Leaders must take action to help you make positive changes in the way you approach your life, career, and personal goals.*

Great leaders don't become great by just cheerleading or comforting you when you fail. Support is a valuable part of leadership, but you can grow only when someone identifies a weak point, shows you why you need to change, and helps you change. Without growth, that person didn't really lead you. They just told you what to do. Often, the harder a leader was on us, the more change they produced and the greater appreciation we feel.

Every successful person has a leader who fills this role, including greats as varied as Jack Welch, Mother Teresa, and Babe Ruth.

I collected baseball cards as a child and still have an extensive collection. Like any child in the '80s, I wanted a Babe Ruth card. In addition to his clout as a hitter and pitcher, Ruth was regarded as a wild man with a reputation for drinking, partying, and having a tumultuous marriage.

This reputation started spreading through the papers when Ruth entered the big leagues. Brother Matthias, a teacher at St. Mary's Industrial Training School, where a young Ruth had been sent by the courts, took off for New York to meet his former student. He arrived at his hotel and invited Ruth to dinner. Because of Ruth's deep respect for Brother Matthias, he happily agreed. Over dinner, Matthias addressed the issues he saw in Ruth's life and persuaded him to change how he lived. Though Ruth wasn't perfect, this meeting marked a pivotal moment in his life. He started to drink and party less and became a better teammate.[6]

Brother Matthias wasn't a boss. He was a leader. He had no way of punishing or threatening Ruth. His influence had grown over the time he spent coaching and developing a young Babe Ruth. That influence was so strong that even in adulthood, he could influence Ruth in ways no one else could. The Babe went on to call on Brother Matthias whenever he needed support. He heavily leaned on Matthias during his career-worst 1925 season and credited him for helping him rebound in 1926.[7]

While I hope you have had a leader like Brother Matthias in your life, I'm not ignorant enough to think you've never had a bad boss. Everyone has been led by people who lack the training, desire, or emotional intelligence to lead well. These bosses are not leaders; they are only managers of people (at best). When you do something for these managers, you do it only because you are told to and want to keep your job. As much as business leaders like to point to quiet quitting as a personal problem, employee engagement is always the leader's responsibility.

Quiet quitting and other forms of disengagement happen when a leader can get only compliance, not buy-in. A boss gets people to do their work because they want a paycheck. A leader can influence people to the point where they are not just doing a job to get a good performance review. They do it because they don't want to let their leader down.

Becoming this kind of leader starts with developing a genuine care for the people on your team. Managers can become leaders only when they provide support and care for their employees in areas beyond what they can do for the company. Real leaders see the company as a way to help their employees reach their personal goals.

Influential leaders want to see people grow! If you don't want to help others grow, don't be a leader. You can make a lot of money and even leverage some influence as an individual contributor. There is nothing wrong with that. But if you decide to make a career as a leader, you must be prepared to invest in others' lives and hold them accountable for growth. Leadership is, after all, the people business. Leaders should be just as passionate, if not more passionate, about their people as they are about their company.

Everyone should evaluate their passion for people when they are considering taking on a leadership position. I once worked with an incredible salesperson who had worked as hard as he could and achieved the highest accolades available in our company. Leadership would be a natural next step, but this employee was more interested in being an individual contributor. He wanted to move into global account sales, but to take that position, he needed experience as a sales manager. For him, leadership was just a stepping stone to a better-paying sales job.

I hesitated to agree to help this employee work toward this leadership position because I didn't think that he was prepared to deal with the challenges people would present. Although he ended up doing well in the

THE TRANSFORMATIONAL POWER OF FEEDBACK

sales manager position, he did not embrace the collaborative elements of leadership. He could manage his team's needs but struggled to lead them in a way that would help them reach their fullest potential. When a spot opened up in global accounts, he bolted from his sales manager job and never returned to leadership.

The pressures of meeting the company's expectations while also caring for people can cause a lot of stress and tension. You have to not only navigate your personal challenges but also support your team members. I have worked for leaders who did not strike this balance well. They spent too much time working on their own goals and left the team to take care of themselves. As a result, many employees did not know what was expected or how to do their jobs well. Because a leader has many extra responsibilities, it can be hard to spend time on the company's goals, your own goals, and your employees and their goals. But if you can strike the balance, it's worth it!

That's not to say that you must have a solution for every problem. After all, you are their leader, not their counselor or pastor. Your job is to serve as a coach working to get the best out of people, which will lead to the best results for your organization. By giving great feedback, you can help them navigate the challenges in their careers, even when they are going through personal difficulties.

Great leaders know that caring about each individual is the best way to have a healthy team. I am the beneficiary of people who took the time to care enough about me and were willing to hold me accountable not only to the goals they set but also to my career and my family. These leaders made the most impact on my life. I would not be where I am without them. As I moved into more significant leadership positions, I decided to do the same for others. I've made plenty of mistakes but have also had plenty of successes. Nothing makes me feel more proud of what I have accomplished than getting a text from a past employee sharing how my feedback helped them achieve their goals and get to where they are today.

I can see the impact of leaders on my life, but I also know plenty of leaders who missed out on their opportunity to make a big impact. Some were too passive in their approach and didn't hold people accountable. Others belittled and bullied their employees into working harder and faster. If a few leaders had such a profound impact on my life, what would our companies and our world look like if we could equip more leaders to carry this level of influence?

Understanding the power of feedback compelled me to leave my corporate job at the company where I had spent nearly twenty-five years of my professional career to start my own company. Today, I train leaders to give compelling feedback to the people on their teams. As you engage with this book, I firmly believe you will learn how to earn the right to give feedback, navigate feedback conversations confidently, and provide accountability.

Even if it feels awkward at first, people are counting on you to help them achieve their dreams.

Reflection Questions

Which three leaders have made the most significant impact on your life? What about them inspired you to trust them and want to listen to what they had to say?

Describe the best piece of feedback you've ever received. Why did you listen to the person giving you feedback?

Application Activity

Write a letter of thanks to one of the leaders who impacted your life. If they are no longer alive, write a letter to their spouse or one of their children. Practicing gratitude will help you internalize the importance of good feedback and allow the leader or their family to understand the impact their legacy continues to have.

CHAPTER 2

Your Feedback Inheritance

As much as you may try to avoid feedback, it has been a part of your life since you were an infant.

When you were born, you learned that when you cried, you would be picked up, cuddled, and fed. As you grew older, you received positive affirmations when you learned a new skill like crawling or walking. Eventually, you started to learn that behaviors like cleaning up your toys could lead to rewards, while hitting your sibling would lead to unwelcome consequences.

All of the feedback you received as a child helped you learn about your environment. Children naturally look to adults to provide feedback about what is safe and acceptable. Ideally, with practice, parents learn how to set and enforce boundaries and consequences with compassion and understanding. However, some parents never saw an example of how to give great feedback and adopt their own feedback style. As a result, they take a hard line and attempt to control everything their child does, imposing strict consequences if they don't comply. Other parents try to avoid confronting their kids about what they need to change, leaving them feeling lost and without direction.

I saw firsthand what happens when children don't receive feedback from their parents. My own parents were often too ill or preoccupied to talk to me about what I should or shouldn't be doing. As a child, I got away with disrespecting my parents, breaking curfew, and getting so angry I destroyed walls and furniture with few if any consequences. As I got older, I became increasingly disinterested in any activity where I could receive feedback, preferring to work odd jobs or hang out with my friends.

When I did find someone willing to give me feedback, I pushed them away. The lack of feedback in my life had made me uncomfortable listening to authority figures. The summer before ninth grade, I went to a basketball camp led by the high school coach. He ran us through drills and then started a scrimmage. I was naturally athletic and competitive, so I did whatever it took to score points.

To my surprise, the coach started to call me out. "Hancher!" he yelled. "You've got to get rid of the ball. This isn't street ball!"

I wasn't used to getting feedback, so I immediately bristled. *What do you care?* I thought. *As long as I'm scoring, you should be happy.* After his comments, I decided it wasn't worth trying out for the high school team.

I remember him pulling me out of study hall and saying, "I see you didn't sign up for the team. One of the things I've noticed in the short time I've known you is that you don't take feedback well. I'm sure you have reasons for it. But I felt like I had to tell you that if you don't join the basketball team, it will be one of the biggest mistakes you make. Until you get rid of the chip on your shoulder, my concern is that the things that aren't going well for you will only get worse. You're a talented athlete, and I think you could help the team win. But I think being on the high school team will help you even more off the court."

He was right. I think I could have avoided a lot of bad decisions and made better friends. He was also right in that not joining the team remains one of the biggest regrets of my life. I wish I would have been more open to his feedback. If I had been willing to take his correction and join the team anyway, I might have avoided some of my worst decisions.

I think that's why so many people list a coach as one of the leaders with the most significant impact on them. Coaches can completely transform people's lives because of how much time they spend with their players. They get to know their physical abilities as well as their personalities. Like a boss, a great coach will take the time to get to know their players and determine how to motivate them to be their best. For many, their coaches are the people who taught them how to win and lose gracefully, work as a team, and push themselves beyond their limits.

Many memorable coaches have found a balance in leadership where they can tailor their approach to reach each player. They focus on coaching the person, not just the position. However, some coaches have reputations for being not only firm and direct but also aggressive to everyone. Many college coaches have come under fire from outsiders for their in-your-face approach, even while many of their players and former players defend their methods and express great appreciation for how they were led.

Businesses can suffer the same effects. Every company has its own culture and values that it seeks to uphold. Those standards provide structure to the approach leaders within the company will take toward feedback. You learn the culture by receiving feedback from your boss and observing how others give and receive feedback.

As a young leader, I was impressionable. I noticed that my leaders were very direct and aggressive when giving feedback. When I used that style, it felt unnatural. But I didn't know what other strategy to use to get results. I wanted success, so I copied what I saw. Like most new employees, I did not want to rock the boat and tried to fall in line with the established culture.

If companies are wise, their culture will be upheld by a leadership brand that pushes people to reach their goals while taking a genuine interest in their employees. When companies push for results at any cost, however, they can create an expectation that makes leaders think they must take a more aggressive approach to feedback. In either case, leaders promoted internally will likely take on the leadership style of their boss and reinforce that corresponding feedback style within the company.

The problem with adopting the feedback style you were conditioned under at home, school, sports, or work is that feedback is not one-size-fits-all. Because of the way I grew up, I developed a very competitive nature. I couldn't control much about my life, but I could control how hard I worked. As a result, I put all my energy into winning when given a challenge at work. One November, I was working with my team to come in first place in a competition between the branches of our company. According to the latest email, we were falling behind on sales. If we didn't change something soon, it would be impossible to keep up.

At 5 p.m. I called one of the supervisors on my team into my office to talk about what we were going to do to get back on track. I gave him feedback about how we were doing, ordered takeout for us both, and spent the next few hours laying out a strategy that detailed how to make up ground in the competition.

The problem wasn't just that I made my employee stay late; it was also the night before Thanksgiving.

The next week, my employee came into my office and told me that he did not appreciate my approach. He was willing to work with me, but if I made him stay until 9 p.m. again, he would look for somewhere else to work.

To me, this was normal. I wanted to win. I had received word that we were losing and wanted to immediately work to make corrections. The night before Thanksgiving did not hold any special meaning to me, so I imagined that my employee would not care either. I made the mistake of assuming that the way I give and receive feedback would work for someone else. This is why leaders need to be aware of how they have been conditioned to give and receive feedback so they can understand their tendencies and choose the most appropriate approach.

Conditioned Feedback Styles

The ways we tend to provide feedback based on how we have been influenced can lead to problems. Those approaches include passive feedback, aggressive feedback, and passive-aggressive feedback. Let's take a brief look at each one.

Passive Feedback

Passive feedback often looks like an absence of feedback. Leaders who use passive feedback are the first to look for an escape when there is a conflict. If they happen to stick around, these leaders will push for peace at all costs. Passive leaders prefer to give positive feedback to encourage their team members. They will try to cheerlead their team to do more things that promote productivity. These leaders will not provide corrective feedback unless there is a significant issue.

I have worked with many clients who needed help overcoming passivity in their feedback. My first client described this exact situation. She ran a small company and frequently became frustrated when people did not meet her expectations. Instead of confronting them, she hoped they would solve the problem independently. When months had passed without any improvement, she snapped at the entire team. She hoped that by withholding feedback, she could make her team like her. Instead, they became frustrated by her lack of feedback and even more frustrated when she finally expressed her feelings.

Leaders who take a passive approach see feedback as something inherently negative. To them, feedback produces conflict, so the best way to maintain a conflict-free work environment is to avoid feedback at all costs. As a

FIRM FEEDBACK IN A FRAGILE WORLD

result, they walk on eggshells around their employees. They fear upsetting the harmony they've worked so hard to protect. Feedback is less of a regular rhythm and more of a tool reserved for creating an effect or when failure to address the problem could put the leader's job at risk.

When feedback is required, these leaders will usually lean on the annual performance review to catch up. Because many companies require leaders to give feedback at least once a year, they will take this as their opportunity to try to fix issues. This approach can feel very confusing for employees.

Imagine how it would feel to be a student receiving feedback this way. Your teacher has assigned you classwork and homework all semester. You have turned everything in, studied as hard as you can, and not missed any deadlines that you are aware of. Then, at the end of the semester, you get called into your teacher's office. You are told that you're failing and warned that if you don't pass the final, you will not be able to move on to the next grade. How would you feel?

In business, this would look like doing your job all year and then being told that you were doing it wrong in your end-of-year performance review. Employees in this situation will feel uncertain about the rules for success. Withholding feedback does not protect employees; it makes them feel blindsided when they *do* receive feedback. The lack of clarity and accountability caused by

YOUR FEEDBACK INHERITANCE

a passive approach to feedback leads to increased frustration and disengagement. Usually, employees in this situation will start looking for work elsewhere.

Aggressive Feedback

Aggressive leaders tend to rely on the authority of their title to get employees to comply with their requests and rules. This was the attitude of the branch I worked at as a service driver. The only problem was that the most aggressive leaders had the best results! When you looked at the data, the aggressive leaders pulled up the numbers for the entire branch. They were the ones winning awards and being recognized nationally.

If you grew up with aggressive feedback, you may have been conditioned to need a harsh tone to take action. You might view any other approach as weak or ineffective. Perhaps it was a coach who belittled players publicly for making mistakes. Or maybe you remember your boss frequently barging into the office, yelling something like, "Why can't you just do things right the first time?" and then storming out. New leaders who try to copy an aggressive approach will struggle with empathy and active listening because it was not modeled for them. They will see emotions as a barrier to success and encourage employees to keep their personal problems at home. In fact, leaders who tend to give feedback aggressively must be more careful than leaders with any other feedback style. Senior leaders tend to overlook aggressive methods because they get results!

The drawbacks of aggressive feedback become more apparent over time. Aggressive leaders will eventually destroy their team's morale. No one wants to work for a leader who berates them for their mistakes and micromanages every area of their job description. Ultimately, an aggressive approach to feedback will discourage your team and drive your best employees to seek new career opportunities.

Passive-Aggressive Feedback

Leaders who choose a passive-aggressive style of feedback try to avoid the conflict of feedback while still making it clear when people don't meet their expectations. Statistically, we know that most people experience passive-aggressive behaviors at work. A staggering 73 percent report hearing passive-aggressive comments in the workplace, and over half hear these comments at least once a week![8]

Leaders who take a passive-aggressive approach usually have mixed feelings toward feedback. They don't want to sacrifice results like in the passive approach, but they also don't want to be seen as a monster like in the aggressive approach. Instead, they try to blend the two by

YOUR FEEDBACK INHERITANCE

sending signals that they are unhappy with your performance without actually trying to hold you accountable.

You may have seen a leader give passive-aggressive feedback by sarcastically commenting, "Thanks for joining us. I guess now we can finally start the meeting," when an employee shows up late.

While some people may use passive-aggressive behavior to intentionally hurt people, most use it because they don't have the skills to be assertive and communicate what they need.

Leaders who take a passive-aggressive approach to feedback will do things that show you your behavior was unacceptable rather than talk to you about it.

I remember sitting in a meeting reviewing changes to the employee compensation plan. Our team was finalizing the details, but I still had a lot of questions. We would also be responsible for communicating the plan to our teams. I wanted to ensure I had all the information and could present the plan with confidence, so I started asking questions. My boss didn't seem happy I had spoken up. It was clear he didn't want to be questioned. Later that week, he "accidentally" forgot to invite me out for lunch with the rest of the team. Without telling me, he communicated that questioning him was unacceptable. If I wanted to be included, I would have to fall in line.

Left unchecked, the passive-aggressive approach will leave employees feeling hurt, frustrated, and uncertain about what is expected. Leaders who use this approach to feedback will see decreased productivity and increased turnover, fear, and distrust.

A Better Way: Assertive Feedback

What feedback style comes most naturally to you? Where do you think you learned it?

The style of feedback you lean into is something that you have inherited from the people around you. Your circumstances determine where you start, but they do not have to determine where you end. The great news about feedback is that it is a skill you can learn, not something you are stuck with.

Many of my coaching clients start on one end of the spectrum or another. Learning your bad habits, making an alternate plan, and getting your team on board with the change takes hard work. However, the results when you commit to the process are drastic. The leaders I have worked with have increased their engagement and productivity and decreased their turnover by simply learning how to give feedback appropriately.

So, what is the best style of feedback?

The assertive feedback style blends the best parts of each of the other styles of feedback. Leaders who adopt an assertive style will set clear expectations, form deep relationships, and hold people accountable. I was five

YOUR FEEDBACK INHERITANCE

years into my career before I met a leader who showed me how to give assertive feedback. Brad was my boss when I was a sales manager. Just a few months into starting that position, I learned that my father had cancer. Within a year, my dad died. When I worked with Brad, I never doubted whether he had my back. He balanced supporting me personally with challenging me professionally.

I remember a time when I was struggling to give feedback to an underperforming employee. Brad held me accountable and asked me where their performance improvement plan was.

I replied that I just hadn't gotten around to it.

He didn't take the excuse.

"Listen," he said. "I know that you're nervous to give them feedback because of the employee who told HR you were discriminating against them last year. I wish I could tell you that will never happen again, but it's possible. You can't control what other people do. But you and I both know this is our policy. Giving her feedback and creating a performance improvement plan is the right thing to do for the company and your employee. How will she grow if you don't help her?"

Brad didn't let me off the hook and ensured that I got over my fear of giving feedback. When he corrected me, I didn't feel upset or frustrated. I felt bad for disappointing him. I knew I was capable of doing what he asked, especially with how much support he gave me. He truly was not just a boss but a leader I didn't want to let down. If I could have worked for him forever, I would have.

In a world where people are more easily offended than ever, we need leaders who look beyond results. It's not enough to meet your goals. We need leaders who can change hearts. You have to reach out to people where they are and earn their trust. As people become more and more distrustful of companies and bosses, you will have to prove that you are not putting on an act. You must be genuinely interested in providing the support people need to succeed personally and professionally. Both personal investments and clear feedback are necessary parts of achieving that result.

> *It's not enough to meet your goals. We need leaders who can change hearts.*

Through my work as a leader and as an entrepreneur, I've uncovered a clear, proven strategy that will help you provide clear, meaningful feedback. Even the most introverted and conflict-averse leaders have been able to adopt these strategies and use them with their teams. With this approach, you will feel free to confidently give and receive feedback regardless of your personality or personal preferences. It all starts with earning the right to give feedback.

YOUR FEEDBACK INHERITANCE

—————— Reflection Questions ——————

What kind of feedback did you receive when you were growing up? How do you think these experiences impacted the way you naturally give feedback today?

What feedback style does your company have? How do you think that style is helping or hurting the company?

—————— Application Activity ——————

Have an honest conversation with someone close to you about how you give and receive feedback. Your spouse, parents, mentors, or even friends should be able to identify your strengths and weaknesses and point out potential blind spots. Being aware of your tendencies in giving and receiving feedback will help you process the information in this book and ensure you know which portions you need to work on.

CHAPTER 3

Relationships Build a Foundation for Feedback

When we left off talking about my meeting with Sean, I was just arriving at his office. My heart raced as I battled a feeling of dread. I was still reeling from the death of my mom a few months earlier, and now I was sure I was heading into the first of a series of disciplinary actions that could quickly destroy my career with this company. As I entered, Sean asked me to have a seat and looked at me with genuine care in his eyes.

I loved working for Sean. He was easy to talk to and willing to help new salespeople learn and develop their strategy. He knew that taking care of my mom had been one of my primary motivations. I had shared with Sean that I used to watch her cut pills in half and that my success meant that she could get the full dose of any medication she needed.

As we sat down, Sean started to lay out my current challenges, both personal and professional. "I know this sucks. It's the worst news you could think of," he said. "I know how much your mom meant to you, and I know your goals were to help provide a better life for her."

Then his tone shifted and became more matter-of-fact. "But you need to remember that you have a wife and a son to provide for. They're counting on you too. And I know you're capable of more. You're a good salesperson. You know how to work hard and be resilient, but I'm not seeing that right now. I've given you time to grieve and plenty of time to gather yourself, but now you need to make a decision. You need to decide if you're going to move forward and do what I know you're capable of doing."

If Sean had been just another guy, this conversation could have gone wrong. I was in a tough spot, heading down the road toward termination. But Sean knew me. He knew my dreams and my goals. We shared dozens of car rides to client meetings, and he role-played cold calls with me until I felt like I couldn't possibly keep going. Sean wasn't just a boss, he was a man I looked up to and appreciated. His words held meaning. I knew he wasn't saying this to be mean or uncaring. He was right. At some point, I had to choose whether I would let myself be defined by my mother's death or if I would keep on living and find a new purpose.

Sean challenged me to be my best, even in the worst situation. He didn't let me give up on myself or my dreams. Every time I have to have a tough conversation in leadership, I think about how Sean helped me and remind myself that I want that opportunity to help other people.

His feedback not only changed my life but also changed my approach to feedback. I used to see feedback as something leaders had to do in order to be compliant with the policies of their company. It was a way to get results and earn rewards and accolades. But, as I continued following his advice and working directly with Sean to improve my sales numbers, I realized feedback is about more than results: It's about people.

> *Feedback is about more than results: It's about people.*

Earning the Right to Give Feedback

I still remember how I felt when my executive assistant, Karen, told me she didn't feel like anything she did was good enough. I was shocked. Karen thought I didn't appreciate her work? This seemed impossible. I knew that I constantly commented to my wife and coworkers about how much I loved Karen and how much easier she made my job.

"What do you mean?" I asked. "You do incredible work. I don't know what I would do without you."

"You never say thank you," she said. I could feel her emotion in the conversation. She wasn't mad, she was hurt. "You're so high-strung. You're always barking orders, but you never take the time to say thanks or appreciate how hard I'm working to try to keep up."

When Karen criticized me for being hard to please, I realized that the deposits I was making into her were not significant for the number of withdrawals I made. To me, I was just giving feedback. It never carried any kind of emotional weight. I was just looking for ways for us to continually improve. But to Karen, the number of corrections outweighed the number of positive interactions we had. To ensure she believed that I was happy with her work, I had to work on going out of my way to compliment the things she did well and ensure that my communication did not come off as harsh or unhappy.

You have to make deposits in order to make withdrawals. At the bank, you overdraw your account if you take out more than you have put in. In business, when you take out more than you put in, you create resentment. Employees who feel like you are overly critical or expect them to work beyond their job description will become disengaged and eventually quit. You have to maintain the deposits you make into your team so they

RELATIONSHIPS BUILD A FOUNDATION FOR FEEDBACK

develop a level of trust that will allow you to call them to a higher standard when necessary.

Leaders can fall into a bad habit of making too many withdrawals from their people. Why? Is it because they are negative? Is it because they really don't think that anyone is good enough? No! As a leader, you are hard-wired to look for problems and fix them. Problems cause us stress, waste our time, and lead to us missing our goals. By fixing problems, we receive positive feedback from our peers and boss and feel good about our contribution to the company. The reward for fixing a problem is also immediate. It feels good to make progress and eliminate barriers to success!

But because we focus on eliminating problems, we can fail to recognize success.

Employees who consistently turn in their reports on time are contributing a lot to your team. But because it is expected, we don't usually take the time to recognize that work.

One of the worst performance reviews I ever got was because of this tendency.

I received a two out of four for leadership.

I was shocked. My team was exceeding expectations. No one was quitting, crying in my office, or complaining about me to other managers.

"I know this is a shock to you. And I want you to know no one is gossiping about you behind your back,"

Sean said. "I've just been doing this for a while, and I know the questions to ask. Your team respects you. But you aren't doing a good job making the investment you need to. I'm giving you a two because you need to understand how serious this is. You can get by with this approach for now, but it is going to limit your potential."

I nodded along, processing, trying to understand what to do differently.

Sean reached into his pocket and pulled out three fifty-cent pieces.

"You're a driver. You see the problems. That's why I want you to put these in your right pocket. Your day doesn't end until you move all three of them to your left pocket."

I took the coins from him and put them in my pocket.

"You move a coin when you catch someone doing something right and talk to them about it. That's three deposits a day, fifteen every week."

I took the challenge and started catching people doing things right. Some days, I moved all the coins before lunch. Other days, I was calling people on my drive home. But Sean's feedback helped me build the habit of calling people out for what they were doing well.

This is also why the regular one-on-one meeting is so critical. Every time you ask someone about their

RELATIONSHIPS BUILD A FOUNDATION FOR FEEDBACK

personal life, help them reach a goal, or invite them to give their perspective, you're making a deposit. I recommend leaders schedule these meetings weekly so that they never go a week without making a deposit.

I'm still not perfect at this. My tendency is still to push people hard and push myself harder. When I realize I'm not making the deposits I want to, I will go back to this exercise and reestablish the habit. I check in with my team and ask for feedback, and I listen to it.

When Karen gave me feedback on how I made her feel, it was a wake-up call. The company was in a particularly difficult season, and we were going through a lot of change. I was so focused on moving forward and accomplishing the goals my leaders needed me to accomplish that I was failing to support the people who needed me most. I was making few, if any, deposits. Karen's emotional tank was empty, and it was my fault. I had to take ownership of my mistakes and create systems to do better.

The good news is that there are countless ways to make investments. Company-wide rewards, pay raises, and promotions are only a few of the ways you can invest in your employees. Many of the deposits leaders invest in their employees every day cost only one thing: time. Investments can be made in two main areas: professional and personal.

Professional Investments

Professional investments start with laying the groundwork for feedback. If you have not given your employees a clear expectation, you cannot hold them accountable for meeting it! No one can hit a target they can't identify, and if they do hit it, it's a miracle, not a result of your leadership. Your expectations must be clear, reasonable, and fair.

Imagine if I took you to the track right now and told you that you were expected to run a four-minute mile. How would you feel? Would you be prepared to even try? Some of you might be in shape and willing to try running the four-minute mile, but others would refuse to even start. If we started right now, some of you would be running in a full suit and dress shoes, while others might not be wearing shoes at all.

A leader who understands clear and reasonable expectations will make sure their team has all the equipment they need to succeed. In the case of the four-minute mile, you need running shoes and athletic clothes. Your employees need the software, uniforms, and supplies necessary to complete the job. For a four-minute mile, you would need to offer your team coaching, assistance with their diet, and plenty of time to train and practice before the main event. At work, your employees need to be trained on how to use their

RELATIONSHIPS BUILD A FOUNDATION FOR FEEDBACK

equipment and perform their job tasks. You might need to give them books, additional training, or mentors to help them reach their goals.

I remember moving into a sales position where I was targeting global accounts. I was an accomplished salesperson, which was what qualified me for the job. But what I didn't know is that global accounts are entirely different. The businesses that qualify for this level of sales require a different approach and have different buying influences. I immediately struggled to navigate this new environment.

When I went to my boss to ask for help, he just told me to talk to the other global accounts salespeople. He didn't ask me questions to better understand my problems or offer me any resources, mentorship, or coaching. He made his expectations clear. I had a sales goal to meet, and if I didn't, I would be held accountable. By refusing to give me any guidance, he made those expectations feel unreasonable and unfair. Finally, a fellow salesperson recommended a book that helped me restructure the way I approached global accounts. I was able to get back on track. However, when I was struggling, I was frustrated that my leader did not take an interest in helping me learn what to do.

This leader was not making the professional investments necessary to help me feel supported in my role. Whenever I received feedback from him, I resented it.

How was it fair to expect me to meet a standard without giving me the tools to achieve it?

Earning the right to give feedback starts with setting clear, reasonable expectations and ensuring your team has the tools they need to succeed. If you do not, your employees will view your feedback as unjust and start looking for opportunities where they would be set up for success.

Personal Investments

In addition to setting clear and reasonable expectations, leaders can invest in their people by getting to know them and genuinely caring about their lives. Whenever I took over a leadership position, I would ask all of my employees and their employees to fill out a paper about themselves. This report would detail some of their professional goals and what they were hoping to accomplish in the coming year. I also created an opportunity for them to share one personal goal if they felt comfortable doing so.

One year, I reviewed these reports and saw that one of our salespeople had written down that he wanted to take his girls to Disney World. I never went to Disney as a child, so I didn't have a deep attachment to it. In my mind, this goal seemed shallow. Other employees wrote down things like quitting smoking, losing weight,

RELATIONSHIPS BUILD A FOUNDATION FOR FEEDBACK

getting healthier, saving for retirement, and so on. There are a lot of things you can do for yourself and your family; why was Disney at the front of his mind? I had to know more.

When I visited his team's office, I made sure I had time to speak to this employee.

"I saw that you wrote down taking your daughters to Disney as a personal goal," I said. "Tell me more about that."

He looked thoughtful and began to explain his family situation. "A few months ago, my wife left me. She just disappeared, leaving me and our two daughters behind. I've been trying to get used to being a single dad, but it's been really hard. Every night, I pray with my daughters before they go to bed, and they always pray for two things."

His voice remained steady, but I could see his eyes start to water as the emotion of the moment swelled.

"They pray that their mom will come back and that they will go to Disney World. I can't do anything about the first one. But the second one? I have the power to make that happen for them."

Our conversation made an immediate emotional impact. I wanted to text my wife and tell her we needed to buy this man tickets to Disney immediately. But I also knew that this compelling goal was a fantastic opportunity for this dad to leverage his motivation and improve his job skills. Then a trip to Disney isn't just a onetime gift—it's just a small piece of the wealth he can generate for his family.

By knowing what motivated this dad, I was able to keep that goal in front of him. When he had a bad month, I could point back to the goal as I gave him feedback and remind him why all the work he was doing was worth it. When he had a good month, we could celebrate his success and look for ways to capitalize on it.

Some time passed, and I moved on to a different position. One day, my phone buzzed and on it was a text message. The first thing I saw was a picture of this dad and his two daughters standing in front of Cinderella's castle. Not only did the picture make me emotional but the text that followed impacted me deeply. He went on to thank me for caring about his personal goals and holding him accountable to achieve something meaningful in his life.

This moment was one of the times I remember seeing the influence that my leadership was able to have on someone else's life. By helping him reach his goal, I had impacted not only his life but also the lives of his daughters. When you support people in reaching their goals, you will have the ability to speak clearly into their lives in a way that they are willing to receive.

In addition to knowing their goals, it's essential to know your team's talents and track record. This is

RELATIONSHIPS BUILD A FOUNDATION FOR FEEDBACK

especially important for a leader taking over a new position. The better you know your team, the more you will ensure you are creating a structure that supports them and their goals.

I once worked with an employee who was consistently one of our top three sales reps in the country. At the time, my company had a rule that every salesperson had to come into the office on Monday and Wednesday and cold-call for four hours. After I had been working there for some time, this employee came into my office and asked me if I could hear her out.

"I know the policy is that everyone has to come in and cold-call, but I'm making so many connections and getting so many referrals that spending eight hours a week cold calling is taking away from my ability to chase those warm leads."

I thought about it. I knew that the policy was in place for everyone. Cold calling is an important part of the sales cycle and generating new leads, but referrals are also a great way to find new business. She had been with our company for many years and was so successful I wanted to help her continue to grow her skills and increase the number of sales she was making.

"What if," she suggested, "I come in on Mondays and make calls and say hello to the other sales reps, but I use that time on Wednesdays to work on connecting with my new referrals?"

I thought again about her success, her track record, and her tenure with the company. Was it reasonable and fair for me to expect her to do the same things that new sales reps were doing when she was one of our most successful sales representatives?

"I agree," I said. "You've had so much success. If this is what you think will help you continue to improve, I'm willing to give it a try. You are now officially excused from cold calling on Wednesdays."

She thanked me and got back to work. I had to deal with a few employees complaining about her new schedule. They argued with me that it wasn't fair. But I told them that if they could reach the same number of sales as this employee, they could be excused from Wednesday calls too. Time proved my instinct to be correct. By allowing this employee some flexibility with her schedule, she improved her sales numbers again. If I had insisted on sticking with the policy and ignored her track record, I would have prevented her from growing her skills, and the company would have missed out on the extra revenue her sales generated.

When you know your people, you will realize that you can't treat everyone the same way. Imagine if you gave a new employee the same amount of coaching you gave a seasoned employee. The new employee would likely feel unequipped to do their job well. And if you gave a seasoned employee the amount of one-on-one help

RELATIONSHIPS BUILD A FOUNDATION FOR FEEDBACK

a new employee needs, your seasoned employee would feel micromanaged and distrusted. Some people thrive with frequent check-ins, while others get distracted and nervous. The more you get to know your team members, the more easily you will be able to tell if something is going wrong.

I once helped an employee get promoted to a management job that required him to move his family several states away. He was excited about the new opportunity but also aware of the stress the relocation could cause. We had talked about the transition and the impact it could have on his family. Through my help in reaching his goals, I had earned the right to give this employee tough feedback. I was thrilled when he was promoted, and we celebrated all his hard work together.

A few months into the job, I got a call from one of his branch employees.

"He hasn't shown up to the office in a few days," they said. "I'm really sorry, I just didn't know who else to tell."

Without thinking about the potential consequences, I booked a flight to his office. I knew this employee was a good guy and a hard worker. His behavior was so out of character I knew that something dramatic must have happened. Just a few hours later, I was knocking on his door.

"Jeff," he stammered. "What are you doing here?"

"Can I come in?" I asked.

He invited me in, and the situation quickly became apparent. He was not living a lifestyle that would be conducive to his professional or personal growth.

We sat down, and I started asking questions. I learned that shortly after they moved, his wife took their daughter and moved back to their hometown. When they left, he started making bad decisions, and things had gotten out of hand.

After listening for a while, I knew that I had to dig into the deposits I had made into this employee and give him tough feedback the same way Sean had given me tough feedback.

"I know you're better than this," I said. "I know some terrible stuff has happened to you, but if you keep going, you're never going to see your daughter again. I can get you help, but if you want to keep your job, we have to act now. You can't stay on this path."

He consented, and I was able to get him the help he needed to recover and get back to work. Much like my conversation with Sean, that conversation could have gone very differently had I not earned the right to give feedback by investing in this employee consistently. Today, he and I are still close, and I am privileged to see him continue to thrive and grow his career. I know that if I had not cared enough to go meet him in his darkest moments, his story could have had a different ending.

RELATIONSHIPS BUILD A FOUNDATION FOR FEEDBACK

Making investments in your employees isn't just the difference between being able to give them feedback or not. It's the difference between whether or not people reach their full potential. The more you get to know your people—their passions, struggles, and interests—the more you want them to succeed. Every time I have to have a hard conversation, I remind myself of this truth. By setting and enforcing clear expectations, you are investing not only in your company's success and your own career but also in the future of your employees.

Reflection Questions

Think about a leader who meant a lot to you. What did they do to make personal and professional deposits into your life? What deposit has meant the most to you?

How are you making deposits into your employees? Is it easier for you to give personal or professional deposits? Why?

Application Activity

The best way to get to know your employees is to have frequent one-on-one debriefs. Many leaders use these meetings to check off questions they have about the status of their employees' work, but great leaders use them as opportunities to invest in their employees. If you don't already have weekly one-on-ones with your employees, start creating time for them. If you do already have these meetings, ensure that you are spending time talking about their personal goals. Are they hoping to buy a house this year? Do they want to be promoted? Talking through these aspirations will help you align your employees' goals with the company's goals and increase trust and engagement.

CHAPTER 4

Earning the Right to Hold Others Accountable

Do you remember your first day of work at your current company?

You may have felt nervous about fitting in, excited to get started, or even concerned about how you would catch up to your coworkers. Then, your boss sat you down and told you about their expectations. These expectations dictate everything about your job, from reporting structure and behavioral standards to deliverables and dress code. After a conversation like this, you were probably able to relax a bit and dive into your work. When employees understand the expectations and how to succeed at the company, they feel more confident in their role.

When I joined the sales team at my company, I was told that the expectation was a white button-down and a blue suit. Anything else was considered unacceptable. Imagine our surprise when a sales rep showed up to a company meeting in a black shirt and black suit. He looked like he was ready to either direct a funeral or perform his best Johnny Cash impersonation!

I had to give him the feedback that his attire was unacceptable and set the expectation. After talking to him, I realized he had not intended to disregard the dress code. He was simply unaware of the expectation. His boss did him a great disservice by skipping over this part of the employee handbook and, worse, failing to address him when he showed up to work dressed the wrong way.

Apart from the slight embarrassment of being dressed incorrectly and our conversation, there was no significant consequence to this missed expectation. The employee simply had to change his clothes and invest in a few more suits in the appropriate color scheme. But can you imagine if he was uninformed about a major expectation? What if he was never told that we did cold calling in the office for four hours in the morning on Mondays and Wednesdays? What if he was not taught how to report his sales correctly? What if he was unaware of how many sales he had to make to remain in good standing with the company?

EARNING THE RIGHT TO HOLD OTHERS ACCOUNTABLE

Setting clear expectations is the only way you can have a right to give feedback and hold people accountable. Still, only 45 percent of employees agree that they know what their boss expects of them.[9]

You encounter expectations every day in the form of speed limit signs. When you drive to work or to take your kids to soccer, you see many signs telling you the speed you are allowed to go on each road. If you are pulled over and the officer asks if you know the speed limit, you likely do!

Now imagine that you are driving down a stretch of highway and you don't see any speed limit signs for one hundred miles. Soon you see flashing lights behind you as a cop pulls you over. They inform you that you are going over the speed limit. You protest. There were no signs! The cop shrugs and says that it is not their problem and writes you a ticket. How would you feel?

Having a clear understanding of expectations is the only way to earn the right to hold people accountable. When you got your driver's license, you were taught how to identify speed limit signs and what the standard limit is when a sign is not posted. These clear expectations and your agreement to abide by them are what give the officer the right to give you a speeding ticket if you do not abide by the law. Without clear expectations, feedback is unfair! How can your employees meet your expectations if you do not tell them what they are? Just like speed limit signs reinforce the expectation of a safe driving speed every few miles, you should reinforce your expectations frequently.

When setting an expectation, you must ensure it is clear and reasonable. Leaders miss the mark when they fail to ensure both conditions are true. If you want to hold an employee accountable to an expectation, you have to ensure that it is something they fully understand and can achieve.

I've always been competitive, but the person I'm most competitive with is myself. I'm willing to do anything to win, get ahead, or reach my goals. But I have also realized that not everyone operates like me, and that's okay! I frequently check in with my team members when we are working on a project to ensure that I am setting reasonable expectations. It is not uncommon for me to ask for a project to be completed in just a day or two. I rely on my team and their experience to help me adjust my expectations and set reasonable timelines.

Collaborating with your team to determine what is reasonable is far more effective than just handing them a list of expectations. If you have yet to sit down with your employees to go over the expectations of their role and their quarterly or yearly goals, you have not earned the right to hold them accountable. It is unfair to expect something you haven't communicated clearly. The best way to ensure you are clear is to set expectations and goals with your team.

If you are moving into a new leadership position, start by meeting with your entire team to set clear and reasonable expectations. A group meeting lets you communicate your expectations on dress, attitude, timeliness, and more. Any expectation that applies to the entire team should be clearly explained here. You should also set up expectations for giving and receiving feedback. If your team knows that you expect everyone to give and receive feedback, you can create positive groundwork for a feedback conversation before one becomes necessary.

Then, lay out what your employees can expect from you. What is your leadership style? What is your personality type? What are your strengths and weaknesses? How can they give feedback to you? Whatever you say, ensure you are prepared to be held to that standard.

Once everyone is on the same page, start meeting with your team one-on-one to discuss role-specific expectations and set goals. This is also a great time to build relationships with your team members and get to know details about their personal lives and goals at work and beyond. The SMART format is an excellent way to ensure your goals are clear and reasonable. SMART goals are specific, measurable, attainable, relevant, and time-bound.

To use this goal-setting format, first identify a *specific* goal you want to set. If there is some flexibility, ask your employees what goal they want to start with. When employees have a voice in setting expectations, they see their goals as more fair and are 3.6 times more engaged.[10] A specific goal narrows in on one topic or area of responsibility. For the sake of our example, let's say they want to set a goal around customer satisfaction.

Next, you will want to ensure that the goal is *measurable*. It's not enough to set a goal that all customers are satisfied or that people have a positive experience with your representative. You must find a way to measure it. Many companies use customer satisfaction surveys to provide numerical data. Using this information, you could say the goal is to achieve an average customer satisfaction score of 8.5 out of 10. This goal is measurable because you can compare the average satisfaction rate reported through customer surveys and compare it to the agreed-on standard.

Then, determine whether the goal is *attainable*. Remember that what is attainable for one person may not be attainable for everyone. By working together with your team, you can ensure that they agree the goal is realistic. In our customer satisfaction example, you could work with your employees to decide what score is reasonable. Expecting a perfect 10 out of 10 every time will make your team feel like giving up on the goal if they

EARNING THE RIGHT TO HOLD OTHERS ACCOUNTABLE

have one bad customer encounter, even if it was not their fault. In the same way, holding a new employee to a perfect standard would be unfair, as they are still learning and may need time to grow into their role before they can achieve the same score as a more seasoned employee.

When I worked in sales, we had different standards for new salespeople. We gradually increased the expectations over a year until the expectation was level with the standard expectation for all employees. That standard was the minimum necessary to maintain employment, not the standard for additional accolades or promotions. I always took an honest look at the aptitude of my salespeople. If they were struggling, we did not set a goal of making President's Club! Working together with my employees, we would set a goal that they could achieve if they put in the work and continued to grow their skills.

In the same way, if they were excellent salespeople, President's Club would not be the minimum expectation. We set specific sales goals, such as aiming to be among the top three representatives in the country. Creating a challenging yet attainable goal earns you the right to give feedback.

Unattainable goals contribute to employee burnout and disengagement. Disengaged employees don't value feedback on their performance. Imagine going into a one-on-one meeting with your boss, knowing you will get unwelcome feedback on a goal you know you

FIRM FEEDBACK IN A FRAGILE WORLD

can't achieve. How open would you be to receiving that feedback?

Attainable goals allow your feedback to be high-impact. Sales managers look at the number of new leads their team members generate every week to ensure they are creating the volume necessary to reach their sales goals. When a leader in this situation notices that an employee has not been generating enough leads to reach their goal, the leader can instruct them to spend more time cold calling. In this situation, the manager is connecting their feedback to the goal and showing the employee how to reach it. Feedback intended to redirect a certain behavior can cause frustration if the employee feels they cannot reach the expectation, but feedback on goals employees believe are attainable produces confidence. When people feel confident that they can achieve their goals and understand that feedback isn't an attack—it's an opportunity for them to improve.

Once you have determined that a specific, measurable goal is attainable, you must ensure it is *relevant* to their role. Having a salesperson develop a new procedure for identifying decision-makers in large companies could be very valuable to your team. However, you must determine whether the goal is relevant to their role. When leaders encourage employees to chase goals not directly relevant to their job descriptions, these goals quickly get pushed to the back burner when tasks more closely related to their job description pop up. It is hard to keep even the most exciting project top of mind when the day-to-day needs of your job pile up.

When you give feedback on relevant goals, your employees know that your goals are aligned with theirs. They can see the impact of their goal on the organization, the team, and their role. If your feedback is on an irrelevant goal, they are less likely to take it seriously, and you look like a leader who is nitpicking their performance.

Lastly, make sure the goal is *time-bound*. Over what period are you measuring customer satisfaction? One quarter or an entire year? How long will it take your employee to create and implement the policy you agreed on? Tasks generally fill the time we allot to them. If you give your employee a flexible amount of time, you will find that the task takes longer than if you set a specific time limit. You can always use your judgment to determine whether you need to modify the goal or the timeline if something more pressing arises.

Time limitations also support your feedback by adding a level of urgency. If you want to rewrite the employee handbook in three months, timely feedback is necessary to keep the project moving forward. Without time limitations, feedback is easily pushed off and forgotten until the leader decides they want to see results. Moving forward without clear deadlines will make you look like a dictator. Employees can wrongly infer that you base your feedback on your emotions toward the employee or their work. A clear timeline creates the expectation for regular, unbiased feedback.

After utilizing the SMART template to set goals with your employees, start gaining agreement. Even if you set goals with your employees, they must understand *why* the goals are important. This is especially true for younger generations in the workforce. Gen Z is especially aware of their work's impact on the world and wants to work for companies that align with their values. Ensure that you spend time casting vision around the goal. What benefit does it have for your organization? How is their task affecting the customer experience? What good is your company providing to the world through its product?

Highly engaged teams don't just expect feedback— they crave it. They agree with the mission and vision of the company and want to see it fulfilled. If you work in a volunteer organization, you know this is true. Volunteers cannot be motivated by pay or other perks. Their only incentive to complete their tasks excellently comes from their understanding of the vision. I have spent decades working with churches outside of my work hours, and the volunteers who make the most significant impact on the organizations are those who don't just know the vision but agree with it and desire to see it come to pass.

EARNING THE RIGHT TO HOLD OTHERS ACCOUNTABLE

Like in volunteer organizations, your employees are also motivated to succeed if they see how their role supports their own goals and priorities. Individuals become even more engaged when they realize how their goals benefit them personally. You've probably experienced the connection between expectations and your personal goals without even realizing it.

> *Highly engaged teams don't just expect feedback—they crave it.*

Returning to our speed limit illustration for a moment, most people do what they can to avoid being pulled over while driving. The government sets the expectations for speed, and people obey it because they do not want to get a ticket or have to go to court.

But let me ask you this: When you drive to work, do you know where the police officer sits? You probably do, and if you're like most people, you slow down when you approach that spot and speed up as soon as the police car disappears in your rearview mirror. This is *compliance*! Compliant employees do their work correctly when the boss is around but take shortcuts when no one is looking.

Compliance occurs when people do not understand why the expectation is good for them. When driving to work, saving a few minutes seems more important than following the speed limit sign. But what if you got pulled over? What if when you did, the police officer gave you

FIRM FEEDBACK IN A FRAGILE WORLD

a ticket and also explained to you the consequences of speeding? Imagine what it would feel like to hear a personal story of the time a police officer was the first to arrive at a fatal crash scene involving a vehicle that was driving above the speed limit. How would that affect your desire to follow the speed limit even when law enforcement was not around?

Employees act the same way in the workplace.

When I worked as a service manager, safety was one of our most essential expectations. Our employees spent a lot of time lifting heavy boxes and moving items around the warehouse. I was passionate about enforcing this expectation because when I was a service driver, I had lifted a heavy load incorrectly and severely injured my back. I had to have a complicated back surgery, and I live with some pain from the injury to this day. Anytime I met a new employee or oversaw a safety training, I shared my story. I wanted to ensure that all of my employees understood that the policy was not created to cost them time. The policy existed to protect them from the pain and lifelong issues I went through.

If you can get your employees to understand how the policies, goals, and expectations you set are good for them, you have earned the right to provide feedback. Instead of the policy being a decree from a pencil-pusher at the top of the company, it is a valuable key to your employees reaching their own goals.

Much of the resistance to feedback is based on a misunderstanding of its purpose. By clarifying your expectations, you can clarify the purpose of the feedback. Leaders do not give feedback to exert power or control over their employees. Feedback is not given out of emotion or frustration or as an excuse to start the disciplinary process. True feedback comes from a leader's desire to see employees achieve their goals. It is designed to keep people safe and promote individual growth while supporting the company's goals. If you want to earn the right to give feedback, you must start by ensuring your expectations are clear and reasonable and that people understand their purpose.

Questions to Ask Yourself to Ensure You Have Set Adequate Expectations

- Are my expectations crystal clear?
- Are my expectations reasonable and fair?
- Has the employee received adequate training?
- Are they facing obstacles to perform as expected?
- Do they understand why it is important to do the job correctly?

Reflection Questions

Has there ever been a time when a problem arose because you were unaware of an expectation? Do you think the outcome could have been different if the leader had set clearer expectations? Why or why not?

What motivates you to complete your goals? Do you have any professional goals that support your personal goals? How do the two tie together?

Application Activity

Create a chart that shows each employee's goals. Then, create three columns. One column should detail how the goal is good for the employee, one should show how the goal is good for the company, and the last should show how the goal is good for the customer or community. Try to fill in all three columns with your employees so they can see the bigger picture.

EARNING THE RIGHT TO HOLD OTHERS ACCOUNTABLE

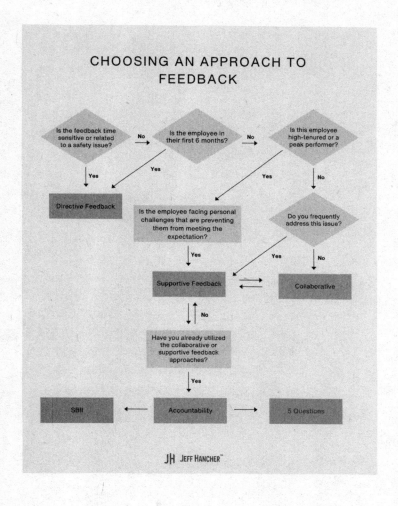

CHAPTER 5

Clarifying Misunderstandings About Feedback

I remember the first time I had to give feedback to an employee. I was still a new leader, and I was trying to figure out how to balance relationship-building with accountability. My team was made up of people I had once worked with and who taught me how to be a good service driver. Coming down hard on the team quickly backfired, so I shifted to a passive approach. Instead of giving feedback and providing accountability, I would try to leverage our relationship. I'd say things like, "If you could turn your reports in on time, it would really help me out." But over time, I saw that my employees stopped responding to these requests.

My passivity started to show as the team's results slipped below what they had been before I was hired.

My boss began to put pressure on me to change this situation and to address one employee about missing his reporting deadlines.

As I realized I had to have a tough conversation with this employee—let's call him Tom—I started to feel sick to my stomach and could barely focus on my work in the hours leading up to the meeting. I had never held this level of responsibility before. How would he respond? Would he be mad? Would he quit? Would he complain to the other employees?

I wondered what to say and how I would even begin to tell this employee that he had to change his behavior. No one had taught me how to give feedback; they'd only told me that I needed to do it.

Has this ever happened to you?

We know that leaders often develop unhealthy mindsets toward feedback based on their past experiences. If you find yourself feeling intimidated about giving feedback, it is helpful to start by ensuring you have a clear understanding of what feedback *is* and *is not*.

Feedback Is Neutral

As defined earlier in this book, feedback is the process where information is returned or communicated with the intent of modifying the next action.

Does that sound positive or negative?

If you said neither, you're right! Feedback is neutral. When you give feedback, you are not passing judgment or accusing someone. You are communicating information.

Sometimes, feedback seems emotional because the leader is emotional. Many leaders respond emotionally during feedback conversations either because they are upset about their employee's mistakes or because they feel like their concerns are not being taken seriously. Emotional leaders will often default to extreme language that labels the employee rather than the behavior. When you label an employee, you say things like, "You never show up to our one-on-ones on time," "You always throw your coworkers under the bus for your mistakes," or "You don't care about anyone else's time."

However, these extreme statements are rarely true. Even if they are true, using emotional language sets your employees up to become defensive. Instead of attacking the behavior, they feel like you have attacked them as a person.

The leaders with the greatest impact are leaders with the greatest composure. They do not allow emotions to affect how they give proper feedback. Labeling a person's behavior or making assumptions about what they meant by their actions will be much less effective than simply describing the situation. Use specific language to describe what the employee did and the impact it made. Remember, feedback is just data. You can be tough and hold people accountable without attacking the person. Your role is to diagnose the problem, not the person. You should aim to be hard on expectations but soft on people. You can make your point without aggression or exaggeration.

Feedback Reinforces or Redirects

The data provided in feedback serves to either redirect or reinforce a behavior.

When you think of feedback, you're probably imagining being redirected. This version of feedback is used when someone is not meeting a set expectation. You might say, "You were five minutes late to today's meeting" or "You turned in your weekly report late two weeks in a row." The data indicates that you did not meet the expectation. From here, a good leader will reiterate the expectation and discover whether there was a misunderstanding or extenuating circumstances. By the end of the conversation, both parties should understand the expectation and the employee should be prepared to meet it.

As much as we want these conversations to feel neutral, people often feel demotivated by what they perceive as negative feedback. Researchers have found that it takes at least five positive interactions to compensate for one negative one.[11]

CLARIFYING MISUNDERSTANDINGS ABOUT FEEDBACK

Leaders can use reinforcing feedback to highlight behavior that meets or exceeds expectations. They often forget about this kind of feedback by focusing on problem-solving. For this kind of feedback, you might say, "You improved your closing rate from 10 percent to 15 percent" or "Your customer satisfaction scores were in the top 10 percent of the company." You should feel free to celebrate employees when you give this kind of feedback! Positive emotion is always welcome and can help people see that you are on their side and happy to see them succeed. The more you recognize a positive behavior, the more they will exhibit that behavior.

Many young leaders are taught to use the *feedback sandwich* to ensure their negative interactions don't outnumber their positive interactions. In my leadership workshops, these leaders will often bring up how this approach helps them give feedback.

I love when my participants bring up the feedback sandwich on their own because it allows me to drive this point home. The idea is that you give one positive comment, then share the correction you are trying to make, then follow it up with another positive comment. It can look something like this:

"Tara, you are an excellent employee. You're always so caring for others, and I really appreciate how you helped with Pat's workload when he was on paternity leave. But you're frequently late. It really hurts the team when you're not on time for meetings. We have to either start late or fill you in on what we already discussed when you arrive. I know you're going to figure out how to be more on time. Your reports are always flawless. You're really bright, and we're glad you're on the team!"

This approach seems innocent, but it is actually manipulative. Feedback should never be used to manipulate your employees. It should always be used to present the facts about how they are performing.

Two things happen when leaders use the feedback sandwich.

First, your intent is unclear. Instead of narrowing down the main issue and providing feedback that will lead to change, you brush over the issue, quickly following it up with a compliment. People will wonder how serious the issue is. If you are happy with Tara's quality of work and her teamwork, how problematic is being late?

Tara likely feels confused about where she stands and what she needs to do next.

The other thing that happens is you create a pattern for negative feedback.

Behavioral scientists call this *conditioning*.

You may be familiar with the well-known Pavlov's dog experiments. Ivan Pavlov gave his dogs a treat every time he rang a bell. When the dogs received the treat, they began to salivate. When this experiment was repeated, the dogs started to salivate in response to the bell, not the

CLARIFYING MISUNDERSTANDINGS ABOUT FEEDBACK

treat! Even when the food was not presented, the dogs produced saliva in anticipation of it. Pavlov conditioned his dogs to respond to a new stimulus that would not normally elicit that response.[12]

When you lean on the feedback sandwich to address unmet expectations, you start to condition your team to expect a negative comment every time you give them a positive one. Then, the emotions that come when people receive negative feedback, like fear, distrust, and defensiveness, appear when they are given a compliment. Instead of being able to accept positive feedback for what it is, your team will be bracing for the other shoe to drop. Let your positives be positive, and your negatives be negative. The deposits you make into your team are what will allow you to make big withdrawals.

Feedback Is a Skill

Your best course of action is to get better at the skill of giving feedback. Just like riding a bike or learning a new language, giving feedback is a skill you can improve with time, study, and practice. No one is great at giving feedback right away. If you are in a leadership position, someone put you there because they believe in you. You have a team of people relying on you to lead them

> *Giving feedback is a skill you can improve with time, study, and practice.*

well, and the success you can help them achieve by giving great feedback is worth the effort!

Throughout my first few years as a manager, I tried many different approaches to feedback, progressing from aggressive, to passive, and finally to assertive. Every time I gave feedback, I learned more about what it takes to set clear expectations and hold people accountable in a way that they can receive.

I wish I could tell you that when I gave feedback to Tom about turning his reports in late he was understanding and quickly made the necessary adjustments. At first, he became upset and asked me why I thought I had a right to tell him what to do. It was uncomfortable. But I knew that feedback was a necessary part of his growth and that if I didn't give him feedback, I would be doing a disservice to him, myself, and the company.

I kept working on my feedback skills, and over time, I improved. I removed my emotions from the conversation, presented the data, and told them where they could improve, and I looked for opportunities to acknowledge what people were doing well. Tom and the rest of the team started to realize that I wasn't giving feedback to be a jerk. I was simply holding them accountable for the agreed-on expectations.

Feedback is the key to growth, both personally and professionally, and leaders have the responsibility to invest in learning how to give meaningful feedback. But

CLARIFYING MISUNDERSTANDINGS ABOUT FEEDBACK

even with an understanding of what feedback is, many leaders have mindsets and concerns that keep them from giving good feedback. Before tackling the specific techniques involved in effective feedback, you must overcome any mental obstacles to implementing those techniques.

Reflection Questions

How did you define feedback before you read this chapter? How does your definition compare to the one in this book?

How have your feedback skills improved throughout your life and career? Consider how you give feedback to your children, spouse, or coworkers.

Application Activity

One of the best ways to ensure that your feedback is neutral is by presenting data anytime you give feedback. Go over your expectations for your team and determine what data you could present to address an employee underperforming in one of those expectations. Having a clear idea of what you are looking for and how to present it before you have to give feedback will help you identify when to give it and how to do it without emotion.

CHAPTER 6

FEAR

The Four Reasons Most People Avoid Giving Feedback

I can't even imagine what my life would be like if Sean had not pulled me into his office after my mom died and helped me rediscover my motivation.

I might have come to my senses, but only after switching companies or careers entirely. At worst, I could have complied with Sean's request and felt satisfied by meeting the minimum requirements to stay employed. Neither of these alternatives would have helped me become the husband, businessman, or friend I am today. To some, his feedback may have seemed harsh or unfair, but because of our relationship and the effort he put into helping me be a successful salesperson, it changed my life.

FIRM FEEDBACK IN A FRAGILE WORLD

Instead of returning to what was easy and familiar, Sean encouraged me to keep going and set new goals for myself and my family. I'm so thankful that he was willing to have that tough conversation. I was at a fragile point in my life. However, because Sean knew how to earn the right to give feedback and follow through on accountability, he made a significant impact. He not only changed my life but also has been a part of changing the lives of all the people who have ever reported to me, and even you, reading this book!

The impact feedback has made on my life has convinced me that it is one of the most essential tools leaders have for influencing their companies and, even more, their employees. Feedback is not about you—it's about the people who rely on you to help them grow and meet their goals.

Imagine having a child who loves candy, like most children do. Being a generous parent, you give your child sweets as rewards and dessert every night. But one day, you take them to their first dentist appointment and find out that they have cavities. The dentist warns you that if you continue to allow your child to have sweets nonstop, even if they brush their teeth regularly, you are putting them at risk for more and more severe cavities.

What do you do?

If you truly love your child, you change course. You find a new reward system and dramatically cut down the sugar they get. Are they going to like this? No! They love sugar. It tastes good, and it makes them happy. However, your responsibility as a parent is to care for your child and ensure you do what is best for them.

Now, think about your business. Imagine that you have an employee named Mariah. She is married, runs marathons for fun, and has two kids who play soccer. She wants to be promoted in the next few years so she can afford to send her kids to private school. But you've noticed she is turning in subpar work and seems to struggle to complete her projects on time. You know that if she continues, she will not only fail to be promoted but may also lose her position at the company.

What do you do?

If you genuinely care about Mariah and want to see her provide a better life for her kids, you give her the feedback.

So why does this feel like a more challenging decision than the dentist example?

For one thing, Mariah isn't a child. She is an adult who is capable of making her own decisions. She could get defensive, cry, or have any number of emotional responses. She could complain that you don't really care about her and then take that complaint to the rest of the office. She might even claim that you are being unfair and report your meeting to HR.

On a larger scale, your team may not be used to getting consistent, meaningful feedback from you.

They might not like it. Some of the things you fear happening if you give feedback may happen. However, it is still your responsibility to give your team feedback so that they can achieve their goals and help the company achieve its objectives.

If you feel like you may have to overcome some fears to give your team meaningful feedback, you're not alone! A study from *Harvard Business Review* discovered that 44 percent of people find giving negative feedback stressful or difficult.[13] Even people who are happy to give feedback will experience situations that challenge them and produce some level of fear.

Leaders often fear giving feedback for four key reasons. Let's walk through each one, using the acronym FEAR.

Fallout

One of the most common reasons people avoid giving feedback is because they do not want to deal with the fallout if the employee quits. Losing a team member will cost you time, expertise, and productivity, regardless of how good the labor market is. Even if you could get a new employee in the next day, you would have to take time to train the new employee and bring them up to speed. Many leaders decide they would rather have a less effective employee than either a new employee or no employee at all.

Additionally, companies under financial stress may treat job openings as a way to reduce payroll. Those that do this will reallocate the work of one employee to the rest of the team. This practice hurts the team that sticks around and makes leaders less willing to enforce their standards and policies because they fear losing a role on their team.

Employees also create drama when they quit, whether they intend to or not. People's attitudes toward their leader are often magnified by what they perceive to be the reason why someone quit or was fired. If they believe the leader is in the right, they will rally behind them. But if they were close to the former team member, they may take their side and approach the leader with suspicion or even animosity. Emotionally intelligent leaders will be able to identify these risks but may also be less likely to take necessary action.

Avoiding feedback and accountability does not protect your reputation—it will destroy it.

To avoid this trap, leaders must recognize the negative impact of allowing an underperforming employee to remain on their team. Many leaders hope that the problem will get better on its own and that their employees will be self-aware enough to address their shortcomings. Hope is not a plan! When unaddressed, underperformers will cost the rest of the team time and quality of work. Have you ever been on a team where one person was not pulling their weight? It's frustrating! Over time, the rest of the team will despise both the underperformer and the leader for allowing them to continue. Avoiding feedback and accountability does not protect your reputation—it will destroy it.

Emotion

When leaders run through what it could look like to give feedback to an employee, they often imagine some of the worst-case scenarios. What if they cry? What if they get angry and storm out? What if they try to start a shouting match?

Dealing with emotions is a common fear. Any time you give feedback, you risk encountering extreme feelings. There is no way to exert control over others' emotions. Even the most calm and compassionate leader will come across people who respond emotionally to feedback.

Imagine that you work with a team of three analysts. You noticed the same error in each of their reports, so you approach them individually with your feedback. You could be dealing with three completely different reactions in these conversations. One analyst might break down into tears, another might get upset and question why you're so uptight about this particular issue, and the third might respond by accepting responsibility and assuring you that they will pay more attention the next time.

Pretend that you delivered the feedback as best you could for each person. Why did they respond the way they did?

People will respond according to their level of sensitivity, personal stress level, and relationship with you. You should do what you can to be fair and empathetic when delivering feedback. However, you cannot control whether someone feels on edge because they had a fight with their spouse before they came to work. Your job is to deliver the information. You have no control over the way they respond.

This should be a freeing revelation!

Yes, you can speak with emotional intelligence. You can ensure that the expectations for roles are clear. You can show people you care about them. But if you have done what is necessary to earn the right to give feedback, the way they respond is completely up to them.

I have worked with plenty of people who cry when they receive feedback. Some of the best employees I've had were especially sensitive to feedback. Most of the time, crying doesn't mean that they are weak or a poor fit for the team. In fact, it's often a sign that they are passionate about what they do and who they are. Their emotion shows that they care a lot about what you're saying! When dealing with these people, you must allow them to cry while you continue the conversation.

The biggest mistake leaders make is backing down when they encounter emotion. If you allow emotions to

FIRM FEEDBACK IN A FRAGILE WORLD

change your standards, you will find that people manipulate their emotions to take advantage of you. Leaders who struggle with an emotional encounter with an employee will become more likely to avoid feedback that they think will elicit strong emotion.

I once had to correct a salesperson who needed to make calls during our biweekly cold-calling session. Let's call him Ben. I gave Ben repeated feedback and talked to him about his goals and how making cold calls would help him achieve those goals. He seemed to agree with my feedback, but I didn't hear him making any calls the next Monday. When I walked over to his desk, I saw he was busy with other work. I always appreciate the effort, but the rule was that everyone on the team made cold calls for four hours every Monday and Wednesday. He was completely missing the point of the scheduled office time. I invited him into my office and tried to get to the heart of the issue.

"I see that you're not making any calls right now," I said. "Is there a reason why?"

He shrugged and said, "I just don't like making cold calls." I stayed quiet to allow him to elaborate.

When he didn't, I said, "Making outbound prospecting calls is a requirement—"

He interrupted me and snapped, "Well, it seems like we're at an impasse."

I continued, "It's not just a requirement; it's a helpful way to ensure you are generating the leads you need to meet your sales goals. I want to see you succeed, but I need you to make the effort in this area. Is that something you can do?"

He refused to give me a straight answer. It was clear that when I attempted to give feedback, he became very closed off.

"Well," I said, "I want to help you meet this expectation because it is one of your job requirements. If you continue not to make the calls, it will become a disciplinary warning. Is there anything I can do to help you with cold calling? We could role-play some conversations, or I could even hop on a call with you."

He shrugged again. "Not really. I guess I'll just make calls next time."

But on Wednesday morning, he did not make any cold calls.

We repeated the conversation, which resulted in little improvement. Ben still refused to tell me what was keeping him from making calls or how I could help support him. When I issued the written warning, he huffed, signed the paper, and stormed out of the office.

After repeating this process a few times, we reached the point where failure to comply with this job requirement would result in termination. His anger increased with every meeting, but he continued to refuse to engage in cold calling. I asked our HR rep to be present at our final meeting to provide extra support and accountability.

Sure enough, the next cold-calling day, Ben did not make any calls. I called him into my office.

"Ben, you didn't make any cold calls again today," I said. Ben had set his eyes in a fierce determination. I continued. "And we have talked about the consequences of continuing to avoid this task several times, so today will be your last day with this company."

Ben was visibly shaking, not with fear, but with anger. I knew I had done everything I could to help him understand the expectation and correct his behavior. Everything from this point forward was up to Ben to decide. He stood up from his chair with clenched fists.

"Ben, you need to take a deep breath and think about what you're doing," our HR representative, Mike, said.

"Man, this guy is crazy," Ben said, his face reddening. "This is ridiculous!"

"Ben, I think you should sit back down. We can talk about what's next," said Mike as he nodded to the termination papers and pen sitting on the desk.

Ben looked at me for a moment, then lowered his fist, stormed out of the room, and slammed the door. He packed up his desk and left without signing.

FEAR

There were a lot of fears in my mind over that conversation. And some of them came true. I lost a member of our sales team, and I had to navigate talking to one of the most angry people I have ever worked with. Fortunately, I didn't get punched. I considered that a win! But I didn't let my fears keep me from having the hard conversation.

Can you imagine what would have happened if I had allowed this man to stay on my team? If he wasn't making cold calls, he wasn't getting new leads and maximizing his influence in his territory. His poor performance could put our entire team under our projected sales. Other team members could get upset if they realized that I was allowing him a free pass on a universal policy. Besides that, his attitude would eventually start to affect the rest of the team.

Leaders who avoid accountability because they don't want to deal with an emotional response are unknowingly creating more problems for themselves. When worrying about emotional responses, you have to ask yourself what pain you are willing to experience. You can deal with the discomfort of navigating a crying, angry, or aggressive person, or you can deal with the discomfort of a toxic environment on your team and decreased productivity. Both approaches will produce some level of pain or discomfort, but by choosing the pain of addressing the problem now, you can reduce the pain the problem will cause later.

Being an Amateur

What kind of training did you receive when you were first hired to a leadership position?

Most leaders are given training on the relevant product knowledge and expectations for their role, but few are actually taught how to lead. Less than 30 percent of companies provide new leaders with leadership training, and an even smaller percentage provide ongoing leadership training. This explains why 69 percent of leaders are uncomfortable even communicating with employees, and 37 percent report avoiding feedback altogether.[14]

Too often, when employees need to be redirected or held accountable for their actions, leaders are forced to wing it. This lack of training can create a lot of anxiety, especially for newer leaders, and put them in a no-win situation. Either they avoid the problem and it continues to happen, or, based on their limited experience, they try to give feedback and risk it being ineffective or offensive.

Leaders with a strategic approach to feedback, on the other hand, are more confident and willing to give feedback regularly. When I was hired into my first leadership position, I frequently reached out to my sales mentor, Dan Billie, on when and how to have difficult conversations. He was a sales leader and gave excellent advice on how to address my employees when they didn't meet my expectations. The more I used his suggestions, the more comfortable I became. I started to build confidence that I could give effective feedback without making people threaten to quit. To this day, I use many of the techniques he taught me.

Since then, the company I worked for has implemented an excellent leadership training strategy. They actually start training and mentoring aspiring leaders before they are hired into a leadership position. I worked with a low-tenured leader on this very issue. She was in our leadership trainee program, and we had many conversations about how to give feedback. Though she was an excellent salesperson, she had a soft voice. She also didn't like conflict, and I was concerned about how these two traits would affect her ability to lead.

Eventually, she was hired as a sales manager. Before her first day, we reviewed our procedures and the key things a leader needs to do to earn the right to give feedback. To her credit, she ran with it! Even when she felt uneasy about an upcoming conversation, she applied what she had learned and followed through. The training made all the difference for her!

I have seen over and over again the positive impact that adequate training can have. My coaching clients often tell me that no one taught them how to give good feedback. They admit that their reluctance to give feedback was primarily based on feeling unequipped and unsure what to say or do. Once they learn the skills, they feel increasingly confident putting them into practice. And repeated practice makes them more and more comfortable.

The key to overcoming a fear of giving feedback is to get over the anxiety that comes with feeling like an amateur. If your company is not giving you training, practice the techniques in this book or seek out online or in-person leadership training. You can only get better through learning and practice.

Retaliation

Have you ever seen a famous athlete or entertainer attacked for a social media post they made as a teenager? The court of public opinion can greatly influence the way others see you. And when enough vocal people think the same thing, they can ruin someone's reputation, even over a simple mistake or misunderstanding. When every mistake can be used as a justification to cancel a career, people are less willing to speak out.

Your relationship with your employees is fragile enough without adding someone who is determined to destroy your reputation! As such, leaders are hesitant to give feedback because they fear their employees will retaliate against them by going over their heads to their boss, blasting them on social media, or trying to get HR involved.

In my first leadership position, I led a team of service representatives. My employees frequently had to go into locker rooms to pick up dirty uniforms and replace them with clean ones. This wasn't a big deal because my entire team was made up of men. However, we were trying to incorporate more women into our teams, so we hired a female service driver. After a few weeks on the job, I got a call from one of our clients.

He was furious.

He explained that this female service driver had gone into the men's locker room while men were changing and showering. To him, this situation was completely unacceptable. I was mortified. Not only did I feel bad for the business owner for being put in this situation, but I also felt bad for sending a female employee into that environment. He said that if this happened again, he would cancel our service.

Of course, we wanted our customers and our employees to feel comfortable with the arrangement. After talking over some solutions with my boss and gaining agreement from the customer, I presented the solution to the female employee. She would first knock and announce her presence when she approached a locker room. Then, she would put a sign on the door stating that a female attendant would be in the locker room for ten minutes. She agreed, and the customer had no complaints after her next visit. I felt like I had done a good job navigating this very complicated situation.

That is, until I walked into work one day to find HR waiting for me.

My employee had told HR that I was discriminating against her because of her gender.

I was given a written warning because of the issue and threatened with termination if anyone accused me of discrimination again.

I was horrified at this situation, and I thought through what I did over and over. I looked for any area where I may have been discriminatory or unfair. To this day, I believe I did everything I could to be fair and helpful to both my employee and the customer. I had built a lot of confidence in myself throughout my time in this position, but this situation caused me to second-guess everything I had learned. After all, my job was at stake! It took years for me to fully regain my confidence through practice and conversations with my leaders and mentors and to reconcile that I was taking a justified approach with my employees.

If you fear retaliation from your employees, your fears may be justified. It's not uncommon for disgruntled employees to speak out against their leader. But that

FEAR

cannot hold you back from giving feedback. If you are treating people well, building relationships, setting clear expectations, and giving regular feedback, you must trust that your reputation will speak for itself. If you allow the negative behavior or unmet expectations to continue, you will hurt your reputation with your team all on your own.

I'll also hear people use their schedule as a reason they cannot give feedback. "I'm just too busy, Jeff!" The problem with using busyness as an excuse is that you create more work for yourself when you withhold feedback. In the short term, you may have to redo customer orders if an employee consistently imports the information incorrectly. You may also have to deal with frustrated employees if someone mopes around the office with a bad attitude. In the long term, you will deal with decreased productivity and turnover as both the underperforming employee and their coworkers become more and more likely to quit over the poor work environment.

Regardless of why you avoid giving feedback, you must find a way to overcome your fears through working on your mindset, engaging in practical training, or role-playing conversations with a mentor. The problems you face will not go away on their own. You can decide whether you want to have pain now in the form of a difficult conversation or pain later in the form of dealing with the consequences of unmet expectations. The choice is yours.

The good news is that the more practice you have with feedback, the easier it becomes. I'm not saying I love to give someone bad news or unwelcome feedback, but I do love making people better. That's why I work to surround myself with people who are open to receiving feedback. When you understand the keys to giving meaningful feedback by setting expectations, choosing a feedback technique, and providing accountability, you will find that some of your fears disappear.

Reflection Questions

Which of the four reasons for avoiding feedback resonated the most with you? What feedback have you avoided giving because you were afraid? What were the consequences of avoiding that feedback?

What helps you build confidence in your leadership skills?

Application Activities

When you feel afraid to give feedback, ask yourself what will happen if what you fear actually happens. What if they cry? What if they get angry? What if they quit? Often, the consequences are not as drastic as we imagine in our heads. The consequence of an employee becoming emotional is that they are emotional. There is no long-term consequence. If they quit, you work to find a new employee. If they try to retaliate and you have followed the steps in this book and your company's policies, you will have proof that you did everything you could to help them. By working through the real potential consequences and separating them from the ones you make up in your head, you can feel more confident about your approach.

Busy leaders often struggle to give feedback because they procrastinate. Many other parts of their job can feel more important (and simpler). As a result, feedback can get pushed to the back burner. In addition to regular, on-on-one meetings, schedule time into your schedule to give feedback. Set aside a half hour a few days per week. If you don't need it, feel free to use that time for something else. But this way, you have a clear spot on your calendar so when the need to give feedback arises, you can address it quickly.

————————— CHAPTER 7 —————————

Directive Feedback
When Clarity Counts

If winning a national championship is the definition of success, Villanova's men's basketball program was a failure for thirty-two years.

Villanova was set to face the University of North Carolina in the NCAA Championship game in Houston in 2016. The Wildcats were hunting their first title in three-plus decades, and UNC was hoping to repeat its 2009 success.

The game was back and forth, exactly how avid March Madness fans like it. Every time Villanova gained a point, the Tar Heels matched them. Neither team could pull away. With 4.7 seconds left, UNC's Marcus Paige sunk an unbelievable three-point shot to tie the score. The game looked destined for overtime. Villanova coach Jay Wright called for a timeout.

On their bench, UNC talked about winning the game in overtime, emphasizing that they needed only 4.7 seconds of defense.

In Villanova's huddle, Coach Wright drew up his play, but he didn't have to. Everyone knew what he was going to say. The play was "Nova," which was designed precisely for this situation and which the team practiced several times a week. Unaffected by the roar of the crowd, the intensity of the opponent, or his own pride, Wright's play told the players exactly what they needed to do. It was up to them to execute and make it successful.

They would have to move fast if they were to beat the buzzer. Forward Kris Jenkins inbounded the ball to Ryan Arcidiacono, and the two raced across half-court. Teammate Daniel Ochefu played his role of setting a screen perfectly. All that was left was for someone to take a shot.

Arcidiacono underhanded the ball back to Jenkins, who immediately launched the ball from just outside the three-point line with one second remaining. As the shot sailed through the air, the final tenths expired, lighting the edge of the backboard red. The crowd seemed to hold its breath, half hoping for a bad bounce and the other half looking for a satisfying swish.

The shot was nothing but net. The Villanova crowd released a euphoric roar, and players ran straight into the yellow and white confetti streamers floating down to the court, celebrating their new status as NCAA champions.

I can't imagine the feeling of success that the coach and team must have felt, but I can imagine the position the coach was in.

He needed to quickly deliver an actionable plan to ensure that none of his five players were confused about what to do.

What made his approach so effective?

It was direct: "Let's run Nova."

Directive feedback is used when you need to set clear goals, define roles, and ensure the receiver knows exactly how to do the task. When you use directive feedback, you're not taking a democratic approach. You're not stopping to listen to alternative perspectives or incorporate new ideas. You use directive feedback when you have a clear picture of what success looks like. In Coach Wright's situation, success was hitting a game-winning three-pointer. Timeouts don't last long. Wright didn't have time for discussion. He focused on delivering a clear plan that would give everyone the best chance to succeed.

When Do You Use Directive Feedback?

You might not be calling many game-winning plays for your company, but you will be in situations where you need everyone to know what to do and how to do it. For example, directive feedback is the best approach when addressing safety concerns. If you see someone lifting a box incorrectly or loading top stock without the proper spotter, you must take quick action to ensure your team member's safety.

I often had to use directive feedback to remind my service drivers about our safety policies. I had sustained a life-changing injury because I lifted a heavy load incorrectly while trying to finish work early. This policy was important not only to the company but to me personally. You don't need to ask questions and devise a collaborative solution with the employee when safety is involved. You need to take action to ensure that they are safe, which means giving quick, directive feedback.

You may also need to use directive feedback when you have a time-bound customer demand. Imagine you lead a team that ships out customer orders. You learn that a customer received the wrong order, and to make matters worse, they are threatening to buy from your competitor if you don't correct the situation immediately. If you want to retain the customer, now is not the time to talk about what happened and ask questions about how to improve your process. You must point out the error to your team and lay out the game plan to fix it quickly. After the crisis, you will have time to consider alternative

DIRECTIVE FEEDBACK

perspectives. For now, your goal is to send a corrected order and provide swift customer service.

Expanding your conversations by asking your employees what went wrong or trying to help them come to their own conclusions will cost valuable time in a crisis. You also will risk the employee or team coming to a wrong or incomplete conclusion.

Can you imagine if Coach Wright had just put the ball in his star player's hands and told him to do his best? Coach Wright had over thirty years of coaching experience. He had a responsibility to share his experience and knowledge with his team of eighteen- to twenty-two-year olds.

In crisis situations, directive feedback guarantees the best, fastest outcomes. A study of the difference between participative and directive feedback in 2022 showed that directive feedback in crisis situations creates better outcomes than more conversational feedback styles, especially in familiar situations.[15] Coach Wright knew his players, and he knew from experience the play he needed to call. His experience dictated the strategy, and he made sure the entire team was prepared to execute the play by practicing it regularly.

In both the Villanova play and the shipping example, directive feedback allowed the leader to identify the problem, assign tasks to correct the problem, follow up, and eliminate cognitive overload.

Leaders who have been conditioned to utilize a passive approach toward feedback often hesitate to give directive feedback because they are afraid of looking like a bully. They don't want to cause conflict. Instead of using directive feedback, these leaders will try to solve the problem on their own or downplay the seriousness of the issue. But effective leaders know that directive feedback is not an attack on another person. Directive feedback is just giving a person information about their performance and what they should do differently.

Players don't resent their coaches for taking this approach. They trust them to handle the game and call the right plays at the right time. It's not that coaches are unwilling to talk to players or build a relationship with them. Players just know to wait until they are off the court to have those conversations.

The more investments a leader makes, the easier it is to give directive feedback when necessary.

Business leaders face the same situations. They look for opportunities to support, encourage, and motivate their employees. The more investments they make, the easier it is for them to give directive feedback when necessary. Besides, people want feedback! Most employees want to do their jobs correctly. They constantly look for assurance that they are doing the right thing. By giving them the data

Negative Impacts of Directive Feedback

they need to improve, you are helping the business succeed and your employees grow.

Negative Impacts of Directive Feedback

While directive feedback can be helpful, it can also hurt your relationship with your employees if it is overused.

Imagine that you have been at your job for five years. How would you feel if your manager was constantly looking over your shoulder, nitpicking every mistake, and telling you how to do your job?

Probably not very happy!

Directive feedback is a vital tool, but you should not use it every time you give feedback. Yes, it gets results, but it also can make people feel like they are being micromanaged. Most tasks are not related to safety or time-sensitive concerns, which means that for tenured employees, most tasks do not require directive feedback. I gave a lot of directive feedback as a new leader. Instead of talking through situations with my employees, I pointed out what I felt they had done wrong and gave them clear direction on how I wanted them to do their jobs in the future. Like many micromanagers, I was insecure about getting people to listen to me. I felt unequipped to have difficult conversations, but I needed to get results. So, I stuck with the approach I knew could get compliance.

Over time, employees started to tell me they didn't want to be led this way. If I didn't find a new way to communicate feedback, they would quit. Leaders who rely on directive feedback for every conversation often are compensating for their lack of confidence in their role, as I was. They may feel unequipped to have difficult conversations, or they may be facing pressure from their boss to reach a standard they think they are unable to meet.

What I didn't know then was that overusing directive feedback will kill innovation. If people feel like they are constantly being told what to do, they will stop presenting new ideas and giving their own feedback. If you, the leader, think for everyone, why should your team think for themselves? If you do not create a space where these employees can share their ideas, they will not share their thoughts. They will do what they think you expect: fall in line.

Employees with a track record of success are especially sensitive to this approach and will feel defensive and devalued if you frequently rely on directive feedback. Your team may start to wonder if anything they are doing is good enough for you. If they decide that the answer to that question is no, nothing will be good enough, their performance will begin to match that expectation. Employees will either do the minimum to keep their jobs (quiet quitting) or look for a

DIRECTIVE FEEDBACK

new opportunity where they feel like their work will be appreciated.

Of course, not all employees are created equally, so you will need to understand how much direct feedback each of your employees needs. Directive feedback is an excellent tool to use with a new employee, especially if they have never had a similar role before. Adjusting to a new role and possibly a new company is challenging. The employee must quickly learn the tasks they must complete, how to complete them, who to talk to when they need help, and much more. The first few days and weeks are not a good time to ask employees how they think they should do the job or let them innovate and create their own way of doing things. New employees don't know what they don't know; it's your job to clearly bridge the knowledge gap.

Imagine how it would feel to be doing a job for two or three months only to learn you've been doing a key procedure incorrectly the entire time. It would be cruel to expect a new employee to know all of your company's policies and procedures right away. These employees need clear expectations and quick, directive feedback when they get off track.

And remember, feedback is not bad, it's neutral! Feedback can be reinforcing. You should give a lot of positive directive feedback to a new employee as well.

Positive feedback reinforces the employee's understanding of what is expected and encourages them to continue doing good work. For new employees, this feedback creates confidence and builds trust.

If an employee is familiar with the job but new to the company, you will probably take a slightly different approach. These employees may know the basics of the job and understand the overall approach to take. They may have developed their own methods for performing the details of their role. However, it is still your responsibility to show them how your company does things. Failing to provide enough direction or feedback will frustrate even the most qualified employee. Once you have caught the new employee up on your company's procedures, you can start to utilize other feedback strategies more quickly than with a less experienced new hire.

Directive feedback will not work without making plenty of relational deposits. Just as Coach Wright had poured countless hours into his players and earned their trust before calling that final play, having a strong relationship with your employees will ensure that your directive feedback is not misunderstood as micromanagement or a lack of trust. The stronger the relationship between you and your employees, the more receptive they will be to all kinds of feedback. I stress this aspect of feedback a lot when leaders onboard new employees, but it

DIRECTIVE FEEDBACK

is equally, if not more, important when you are a leader taking over a new team. Contrary to the direct approach necessary with new hires, new leaders should focus on collaborative feedback.

Reflection Questions

How do you feel about receiving directive feedback? Does the idea of giving directive feedback feel natural to you? Why or why not? How do you think the feedback you received when you were growing up affected your perspective toward this kind of feedback?

Think about a time when you received directive feedback at work or in your childhood. How did you feel about the feedback when it was given? How do you feel about it now? What would have helped you receive that feedback better?

Application Activities

What situations in your company would require you to use directive feedback? Why? What benefit is there for your employees to get quick, clear feedback about these situations? Make a list of ways directive feedback will help your employees and of the risks of delaying or avoiding feedback in those situations. Refer back to it whenever you need to give directive feedback.

Prepare yourself and your new hires for directive feedback. When you set expectations, ensure that you set the expectation for feedback! Then, when you give directive feedback to a new employee, they will expect it and know it is not because you are unhappy with them or their performance. Expecting feedback helps take some of the emotion out of it and ensures that employees see feedback as what it is meant to be: data.

—————— CHAPTER 8 ——————

Collaborative Feedback
Building Bridges, Not Walls

Getting a new boss is hard enough, but it's even more complicated when they are promoted into a position you were also interviewing for.

There was a time when my boss encouraged me to apply for the regional leadership position. He assured me it was a slam dunk and that the company's leaders were excited about my potential. I applied, interviewed, and felt like everything was going well.

This made it even worse when he had to tell me I was not getting that promotion. To say I was upset would be an understatement. But I realized that people were watching how I responded. If I wanted to be promoted, I had to take the high road and do everything possible to make the transition smooth for my new boss.

A few weeks after Hannah became my boss, she invited me to dinner. We met at a restaurant and exchanged some pleasantries. After a while, she said, "Jeff, I know everyone has nothing but good things to say about you. I've heard about your work ethic, President's Club awards, and that you were named manager of the year last year."

Everything she said was true. I had worked hard for the last decade to develop my reputation as a salesperson and a leader, and I was glad she was aware of my accomplishments until she dropped the bomb.

"I just want you to know that none of that matters to me," she said plainly. "Starting today, you have to prove yourself."

I felt like I had been punched in the stomach. Not only had I been told I was the obvious choice for this role, but now the person given the job was talking to me like I was a brand-new employee.

Her decision to disregard my reputation immediately pushed me away. Who was she to tell me I had to prove myself? Wasn't my body of work enough?

I'm not sure why she decided to take this approach. Maybe she had been told I had a strong personality, and she was trying to establish herself as the leader. Or maybe she'd had a bad experience with an employee she was told had a good reputation. It's possible that she was

COLLABORATIVE FEEDBACK

trying to motivate me to be better. Regardless of her intentions, I felt defeated before our relationship even started. My wife encouraged me to try to make the best of it, but the next few months did not improve. I continued to succeed, and she continued to respond critically. She pounced on me if I ever turned in a report late and escalated minor errors into threats to start the written disciplinary process. I felt targeted and anxious every day.

I wish I could tell you I chose the high road, but I felt so mistreated that my negative attitude toward her spilled onto my peers and employees. Instead of defending her or squashing gossip, I fed into it. I had loved my job, but her micromanagement and critical attitude made me dread going to work every day.

Just a few months later, I was already actively looking for a way out. I crafted my résumé and was preparing to apply to other jobs. I loved my company and appreciated everything they had done for me, but I couldn't take working for my boss any longer. It felt like I was preparing to go through a divorce. I couldn't see any other way forward.

One day, while considering my options, a good friend who also worked in the company joined me for dinner.

"Hey, I heard the situation with your boss is pretty bad," he said.

"That's being generous," I replied. "I've never had a boss like this before, and I hope I never have one like this again."

"Hey man, that's rough," he said. "You have to promise me that if it ever gets to a point where you think about leaving because of her, you'll tell me."

"Well," I said with a slight chuckle, "consider this me telling you."

His eyes widened, and he put his fork down. "You're not serious."

"My résumé is together. I just have to hit send on the applications."

His demeanor tensed. "Listen, promise me you won't do anything in the next week. Let me make some calls."

I agreed and was thankful to have someone trying to help me find a solution that did not mean leaving the company. A few days later, I got a call from a leader in a different division.

"Jeff, is there anything we can do to get you to stay?" he said.

"I love the company. I just don't think I can take this," I replied. "I don't want to come to work every day feeling this way."

"Okay," he said. "Listen, I don't have any other leadership roles open. But we do need another salesperson in global accounts. If you want it, the position is yours."

COLLABORATIVE FEEDBACK

I barely had to think about my answer. Working in global accounts would mean I wouldn't be leading people, but it also would mean I could gain some valuable experience before moving toward more senior leadership opportunities. Most importantly, I wouldn't report to Hannah anymore.

I agreed, thankful for the opportunity.

The way Hannah gave me feedback played a massive role in the way I viewed my work. Employees become more invested in the company when treated well and given appropriate feedback. They become more innovative and are open to new ideas. When employees feel micromanaged, disrespected, or unappreciated, they disengage. Their productivity and quality of work decrease, and like me, some of them start actively looking for a new job.

When Hannah took over as my boss, her mistake was taking an aggressive, directive approach to feedback. I made the same mistake when I was a young leader. While I'm sure there were some situations where I needed to use directive feedback, I overused it. The most influential people on my team hated me, and if I didn't change my approach, they would lead a revolt.

So, I backed off. I reset the expectations with the team, and I started asking a lot of questions. I didn't let my standards fall, but I changed how I approached providing feedback.

I started using the approach I recommend most when dealing with tenured, high-performing employees: collaborative.

What Is Collaborative Feedback?

Collaborative feedback is a two-way method of communication that prioritizes seeking a complete understanding of the situation and working with the employee to create a solution they can take action on.

In most situations, a collaborative approach begins by listening and not giving directives. High-tenured employees know what to do. They don't need a plan— they need a guide. They need someone who can challenge them and help them improve their skills. They don't need a hand to hold—they need someone who can get them to the next level.

As a leader, you are like a coach. Leading your team requires you to identify areas of improvement, remove roadblocks, and keep the vision in mind. A coach for a sport might give more directive feedback because they are looking for a quick win. In business, an error-free report isn't the most important win. Your goal is to develop successful employees who will be promoted or become well-tenured individual contributors.

COLLABORATIVE FEEDBACK

Instead of giving directive feedback to address potential errors, start by asking questions. This approach is critical when taking over a new team.

After gaining some experience leading my new team, I focused on collaborating this way. In one situation, I needed to make many changes more quickly than usual. Change is hard for most employees, especially those who have worked for the same company for years or even decades. Understanding this, I knew that asking questions and providing empathy would be crucial as I tried to earn the team's trust.

In my second meeting with Paul, one of my new employees, I asked for candid feedback about his expectations and concerns. Thankfully, Paul was forthcoming and vulnerable and admitted that he was concerned about how my reputation as a very driven person would affect the organization's pace.

"We're all so busy already. It's really important to me that I find a good work-life balance," he said. "But honestly, I'm worried you will pile on more work and not respect those boundaries."

I nodded and paused to ensure he was done speaking. "I really appreciate your openness," I said. "The fact is, I probably will add more work. We're a growing organization and you play an important role. But I don't want it to feel unmanageable, and I want to respect your priorities. Let's look at what you're doing and how I can help you find more capacity."

For the next few weeks, I had Paul track how he was spending his time. I made it clear that I didn't want to micromanage his time. I didn't even need to see the time journal he completed. I just wanted him to get a clear picture of his workweek. When he completed the assignment, I asked him what he saw when he looked at the results.

"Honestly, I have a little more time than I thought I did," he said. "But I don't know how much more I can accommodate unless I get some of these tasks off my plate."

I followed up with questions like:

What tasks could you delegate?

What has kept you from delegating those tasks in the past?

Are there any barriers slowing you down or making you feel like you can't delegate these tasks?

In this case, collaborative feedback helped me develop a relationship with Paul and the rest of the team. It also helped Paul recognize ways he could improve. He identified areas he could delegate, and we discussed how I could help make that process easier for him. The goal wasn't to manipulate Paul into doing things my way. The goal was for Paul to determine how he could meet my expectations and what I needed to do for his plan to work well. I also wanted to ensure that Paul knew I

COLLABORATIVE FEEDBACK

was willing to help him in the future if he ever felt overwhelmed or like the workload was too much.

If I had come into the meeting and said, "You're not as busy as you think you are. You need to delegate x, y, and z," I would have created a barrier! I would have come across as if I thought I knew more than the person doing the work for the last five years. My job wasn't to tell him what to do but to help him find ways to do it better.

Some employees may respond well to directive feedback, but most high-performers are perfectionists and become defensive when you tell them what to do. They interpret your direction as distrust and are quick to withdraw or attack. Ideally, you can help employees become better at responding to feedback and take it less personally, but that doesn't excuse you from the responsibility to deliver feedback in a way they can accept.

Directive feedback puts you in the place of the expert and your employee in the place of the learner. This position is more comfortable for leaders who have adopted an aggressive feedback style. To give collaborative feedback, leaders must acknowledge that they don't have all the answers and create space for their employees to do most of the talking. Asking questions ensures you do

> To give collaborative feedback, leaders must acknowledge that they don't have all the answers and create space for their employees to do most of the talking.

not assume anything about your employees, their work, or their motivation.

On the other side of the scale, leaders who lean toward passive feedback may naturally gravitate toward a collaborative style. They feel more comfortable giving people the responsibility of identifying their needs. Their challenge will be to ask questions that will challenge their employees and drive the conversation forward. Questions that help you extract information will be open-ended and curiosity-driven.

Open-ended questions have more than one or two possible answers. If you must ask a question that has a yes or no answer, make sure that you follow up with another question to get more information. For example: Have you been getting the support you need to fulfill orders on time? What specifically has been helping or holding you back?

Closed-ended questions make it difficult to extract additional relevant information. They limit the answers your employees can give and how they think about their answers. For example, if you ask an employee if they feel supported, they might assume that you are asking if they feel supported by you. So they say yes, even though they feel like the rest of the team is not good at working together or offering each other support. But if you ask, "What would it look like for you to feel supported in this role?" you can get a clearer picture of your employee's

COLLABORATIVE FEEDBACK

ideal situation and create an opportunity to ask clarifying questions. Asking open-ended questions shows that you are curious about your employees and want to hear any information they are willing to offer.

Leading questions can also limit the effectiveness of your questions. These are questions where you imply that there is a right or a wrong answer. They sound like this: You're getting good support from our in-house leadership training, right? Other employees like coming to work rather than working from home; what do you think? Questions like these will plant bias in your employees' minds, making them more likely to give the answer they think you want to hear.

When I took over a sales division with a very high-performing employee, I relied heavily on asking questions. He was one of the best salespeople in our company and the industry. Throughout the interview process and transition, other leaders cautioned me to take care of this employee. It was apparent that we could not afford to lose him.

I planned a trip to Atlanta to visit his office and meet with all the salespeople there. I scheduled this person's meeting for last, so I knew we would not have to rush through our discussion.

For days, I thought about how I wanted to approach this conversation. As I did, I reflected on how Hannah treated me when she took over my division. I knew that an aggressive approach would be counterproductive. I couldn't tell him what to do, and honestly, I didn't want to. But how would I establish myself as a leader *and* earn his trust and respect in one meeting?

I thought about my approach on the plane, at the hotel, and even on the car ride to the office. As I looked over his sales numbers and reflected on his reputation as a person, I developed a genuine respect for him. I decided the best way to start the meeting was by being clear about how I felt.

"I've heard so much about you, and I'm very impressed," I said, recounting his recent sales numbers, awards, and accolades, and trying to show him that I understood the magnitude of his success. Then, I started asking questions: What has led to your success? What are your strengths? What needs do you have? I'm new to this service offering; what advice do you have for me to become more familiar with it? The further into the conversation we got, the more I saw him light up. He was excited to have the opportunity to talk about his success and give me insight into what it was like to make sales in Atlanta.

Finally, as I approached the end of my list of questions, I set the stage for the most critical question.

One of the challenges we face when leading high-performing employees is finding ways to help them improve. Leaders, that is your biggest job! Your best

COLLABORATIVE FEEDBACK

employees are often your most perfectionistic employees, which can manifest in defensiveness and resistance to asking for or accepting help. To open up these employees to feedback, you must get them to buy-in.

First, I reiterated my belief in this employee and my understanding of his track record. "To be clear, I'm not asking this next question because there's anything I want to talk to you about right now," I said. "But if I ever noticed something that could make you better at your job, would you want me to tell you?"

He looked slightly taken aback and then said, "Yes, of course. I'd love that."

I said, "I am so glad to hear that. Again, I don't have any feedback like that right now, but I love working with people who are open to feedback and want to grow."

Knowing that this employee wanted to continue to grow let me know that as long as I continued to make deposits into our relationship and genuinely care, I would have an open door to provide feedback.

When Not to Use Collaborative Feedback

Even for a successful or high-tenured employee, there are still situations where you can't afford to use collaborative feedback. Directive feedback is always the best choice when addressing behavior that must be corrected imme-diately, like safety issues and time-bound demands. The shorter the time frame to provide correction, demonstrate exemplary customer service, or achieve a time-bound goal, the more likely you will need to engage in directive feedback.

Leaning on collaborative feedback will ensure that you have a strong track record with your employees when you do have to use directive feedback. The better your relationship, the more likely they will understand and receive your directive feedback without feeling like you don't trust them or are on a power trip.

Early in my career, I remember needing an excellent month of sales to qualify for President's Club. Earning this award came with bonuses and special recognition. It was my goal to qualify for this honor every year. At the time, Sean was my boss, and he was determined to help me achieve my goal. So, we sat down and talked about a strategy.

The solution was not simple. Usually, you focus on chasing as many leads as possible in a given month. But we were in the final month of the fiscal year. For my efforts to count, we had to not only close the sale but also fulfill the order and invoice the company by the end of the month. Sales for uniforms or other products that had to be specially produced would be risky because we couldn't guarantee a quick turnaround time.

After discussing the options, Sean looked at me and said, "Jeff, if you want President's Club, you have to go

COLLABORATIVE FEEDBACK

big or go home." I nodded in agreement. I wasn't afraid of hard work. I was willing to knock on as many doors and make as many phone calls as it took. "Instead of chasing all the accounts in your sales funnel, I want you to go after this one." He pointed to the file of a mining company a few hours from our office. If I could close this sale, I would make more in commission than most of my other leads combined.

I must have looked shocked because he quickly added, "I know it's high risk, but it's also high reward. We can do this."

I pushed back. Chasing one account was crazy. What if they rejected our offer? What if we couldn't fulfill the order in time? What if they pushed us off until the new fiscal year started? I laid out every objection I could think of and presented my plan to keep putting more lines in the water. In my mind, it was better to have more options. If one lead went cold, I knew I had plenty of other options.

He entertained my concerns for a while, addressing them as best he could. Finally, Sean said, "Jeff, we're done talking about this." The time for collaboration was over. We were no longer discussing the risks and benefits. We were no longer sharing notes and strategies. We had the plan, and it was his plan. "The risk is greater the other way. You have to trust me."

I nodded, feeling defeated.

"This is the worst plan," I told my wife when I got home. "I've worked for eleven months to make President's Club, and now I'm not going to get it because my boss insists I use his plan."

After processing my conversation with Sean more, I resigned to accept his decision. That was hard because it wasn't my choice. We'd moved past the collaborative approach, and Sean had given me a direct order. But I knew my boss understood sales strategy. I knew he cared about me and my goals. After all, he was the boss who helped me get back on track after my mom died. So, I decided to put my total effort into his strategy.

Sean helped me in every way he could. We worked on the negotiations together. He suggested preordering the parts so that when the mining company signed the contract, we could move forward with the installation immediately. As the days left in the fiscal year ticked down, he approved additional customer benefits if they signed the contract by the end of the month.

With three days left, they signed the contract.

But the sale wouldn't count until we finished the installation. Thanks to my boss's preparation, we had all the parts in stock, and I was personally invested enough to handle the installation. I loaded a truck with a fellow salesperson and drove to the mining company. We completed the installation ourselves as the sun rose on the final day of the fiscal year. When I got to the office, Sean

COLLABORATIVE FEEDBACK

was waiting for me with our billing department. We sent out the final invoice before lunch.

I made President's Club by the razor-thin margin of $11.

If Sean had used the collaborative approach and let me choose, I would have made the wrong decision. I didn't have the same level of experience, and there wasn't enough time to learn from my mistakes. A decision had to be made, and as the leader, he was responsible for making the call.

The directive approach worked because we had a collaborative relationship. My boss had invested in me as an employee and a person. He was very willing to work with me and ask questions to understand better what I was working through. He was willing to give the support to back up his decision and take ownership. He made calls to give discounts and sweeten the deal for the buyer. He took on the risk of ordering the parts ahead of time. He believed in me and his plan and showed it through his actions.

The more Sean invested in me personally and professionally, the stronger our relationship grew. He had already made excellent deposits when I was a new salesperson who needed to learn the ropes, and especially when my mom died. But his commitment to my continued development and willingness to speak up when needed made a lifelong impact on me. Leaders who learn

FIRM FEEDBACK IN A FRAGILE WORLD

to use the collaborative approach will earn the trust and respect of their employees. Having a solid relationship with your employees will allow you to know when you should use directive feedback, collaborative feedback, or our final feedback tool, supportive feedback.

Questions to Use When Giving Collaborative Feedback

This list is not meant to provide every possible question you can ask, but it will help you start the conversation. Remember to practice active listening when giving collaborative feedback and to ask follow-up questions based on your employee's answers.

- What parts of your job do you love?
- What parts of your job challenge you?
- Why is success important to you?
- What should we stop doing?
- How can we provide better support for you during this project?
- Do you have everything you need to succeed?

Reflection Questions

Identify a time when a boss gave you feedback using the collaborative approach. How did it make you feel? How did the conversation influence your behavior?

COLLABORATIVE FEEDBACK

Have you ever used collaborative feedback? How did the conversation go? What changes did the employee make? Do you still believe collaborative was the best approach? Why or why not?

Application Activities

Think about any areas where you are avoiding giving feedback. Which of the two feedback approaches we have discussed so far would be best for dealing with each issue? Why? If the problem requires collaborative feedback, use the questions above to plan a conversation with your employee(s).

The collaborative approach relies on a trusting relationship between boss and employee. Do you believe your team trusts you right now? Why or why not? If not, how can you use the collaborative approach to feedback to earn their trust? While working on using the best feedback approach, ensure that you are also investing in your employees, as discussed in earlier chapters. Revisit your notes and find a specific way to celebrate the good that people are doing in a way they will be excited about.

CHAPTER 9

Supportive Feedback
Building Confidence Through Encouragement

At just twenty-seven years old, I was asked by my pastor if I would consider running for the board of our church. The board was a group of members who oversaw the church's finances, staff, and other needs. Being on the board was an honor and a huge responsibility, one I was not sure I was ready for.

After our meeting, I called my friend and mentor Dan Billie to tell him about our pastor's invitation. Dan immediately encouraged me to run. He told me he thought I had a unique perspective and new insight to bring to the board. He and his wife were my biggest supporters throughout the process. Much to my surprise, I was voted in. I was told that I was the youngest board member ever elected.

As I walked into the first board meeting, any false confidence I carried melted away. Around a large table sat men mostly twenty years or more older than me. They were doctors, CFOs, accountants, and successful entrepreneurs. At the time, I was a new salesman, just starting my career. I don't remember what we talked about, but I remember leaving the meeting completely defeated and overwhelmed.

Dan clearly had made a mistake by encouraging me to run for and accept this position. Was there a way to resign? Or would I have to go to these meetings every month and feel like I was wasting everyone's time?

On my way back to my car, a voice called out to me. I turned to see a man with a kind smile and a white button-down shirt and tie approach.

"You're Jeff, right?" he said.

"Yes," I said, not sure what he was going to say.

"I'm Joe Bradley," he said. He needed no introduction. He was a well-known physical therapist in our area and an active member of our church. He had an incredible ability to attract the attention of everyone in the room without ever raising his voice.

"How are you feeling after that meeting?" he asked, as though reading my mind.

SUPPORTIVE FEEDBACK

"Honestly? Pretty bad," I said. "I don't know why I was elected to this board. I'm feeling so out of place."

He nodded, ensuring I was done speaking and digesting what I said. "I understand. They can be an intimidating group. But I want you to know that you're here for a reason. We need your passion and unique perspective. I believe in you, and I want to help."

That was the beginning of a relationship I cherished. Dr. Bradley was always ready to listen to me talk about what I was going through and even more ready to provide timely direction and feedback. He knew when to listen and when to correct. He thrived when giving supportive feedback.

What Is Supportive Feedback?

Supportive feedback utilizes active listening, confirmation or praise, support, and encouragement. Leaders who provide supportive feedback focus on identifying and removing obstacles to their employees' success. You might use a little bit of supportive feedback daily, but you will need to use a heavier dose of supportive feedback when dealing with employees facing immense personal or professional challenges.

I remember pulling a salesperson into my office to discuss his recent poor performance. I had been giving

FIRM FEEDBACK IN A FRAGILE WORLD

him feedback and opportunities to improve, but I wasn't seeing any effort on his part to change. I entered the meeting fully prepared to give him a disciplinary warning, which would initiate the termination process if he did not start meeting my expectations.

I jumped into the discussion and held nothing back. I laid out the expectations, showed him where he was missing the mark, and told him that his lack of effort was unacceptable. As I finished my rant, I noticed his eyes welling up with tears. I'm not afraid of crying. I've dealt with many employees who cry when they get unwanted feedback or become overwhelmed. I gave him time to collect himself and give his response.

"I'm so sorry, boss," he said. "I didn't want to burden you with this, but I haven't been myself lately because my wife was just diagnosed with a brain tumor, and it's not looking good."

He went on to say that she had been in the hospital, and he had been splitting his nights and weekends between the hospital and taking on the full load of caring for their children.

I felt horrible. I wanted to throw up. How could I have missed something so significant? He'd given me no indication that there was a problem at home. I quickly realized this employee didn't need directive feedback or a disciplinary letter. He needed someone to show him that there was still a way forward. I immediately

SUPPORTIVE FEEDBACK

pivoted to supportive feedback and started discussing how I could encourage him. We talked through the practical challenges and came up with a plan to help him improve his performance at work while prioritizing his family's situation.

Supportive feedback isn't designed to avoid expectations but to give employees the confidence and resources to meet your expectations.

When you think of supportive feedback, think of a golden retriever. I had a golden for over ten years, from when she was a puppy to the day of her death. I've never been much of an animal person, but this dog had my heart. She was so affectionate and empathetic. When you were ready to play, she eagerly joined in. When you were sad, grieving, or upset, she parked herself next to you and ensured you were okay. In the same way, leaders who give supportive feedback are sensitive to the emotional state of their employees and adjust their behavior accordingly. They choose their words carefully and ensure that they listen even more than they speak.

> *Supportive feedback isn't designed to avoid expectations but to give employees the confidence and resources to meet your expectations.*

Golden retrievers are experts at using their body language to provide comfort and companionship to their owners. You can also use body language and posture to communicate with your employees when you're not speaking. A boss who is leaned back with arms crossed will come across as disinterested or disappointed, while a leader who leans forward and nods as their employee talks will be seen as engaged. Maintaining eye contact approximately 70 percent of the time also shows the speaker that you are engaged.[16] Other meaningful ways to show you care include putting your phone and computer away and clearing your desk. These small actions prove that you are focused solely on the person you are talking to.

Active listening also involves verbal components. Sharing affirmative statements, summarizing the speaker's main points, and asking open-ended questions ensure that you understand what they are saying and receive additional relevant information. Try to avoid moving on to problem-solving or cheerleading until you have allowed the employee to say everything that is on their mind.

When I was struggling with my mother's death, Sean was especially good at active listening. Though he gave me firm direction, he frequently utilized supportive feedback in the weeks and months after my mom passed away. He knew the value of allowing me to feel what I was feeling and assuring me that he would help any way he could.

SUPPORTIVE FEEDBACK

He also used supportive feedback with me the first time I missed President's Club. As a salesperson, I prided myself on consistently making President's Club. The award proved to me that I was fulfilling my goals and leading my family well. But when I didn't make it, I was devastated. Sean helped me remember I was not defined by my performance while also helping me redirect my efforts so I could meet my goals the next year.

Supportive feedback is the best approach when dealing with employees who value success and don't miss their goals very often. Peak performers don't need you to give a big speech about expectations and be reminded of their failure. Most of the time, these employees are already beating themselves up. They need both the assurance that they can recover and the support to get back on track.

You can also use supportive feedback when you have an employee who just needs to vent. Imagine that you are in the middle of a major transition at work. One of your employees was promoted, another quit, and the employee who is left is now covering the work of the entire team. Even with realistic expectations, this employee just lost a lot of their support system. They are learning things on the fly as they try to keep the team afloat. If they want to vent, let them vent! Let them express how they feel. Don't worry about how you will respond until they are completely done talking.

When they do stop, be empathetic. Understand that what they are feeling and experiencing is real. Then, help them find solutions. Look for ways to support them by simplifying processes, keeping the hiring process moving forward, managing expectations with leaders above you, and so on. This combination of empathy and action will make a huge difference in how the employee feels about you and the organization.

Finally, you will often have to use supportive feedback with the *disillusioned learner*. This term, coined by Paul Hersey and Ken Blanchard, describes an employee who is skilled but is not achieving the success they expect from themselves.[17] When you make a new hire, they are eager to meet your expectations. They approach each day with enthusiasm and resilience. But as they gain tenure and experience more difficulties, they begin to wonder if they are really going to be successful in this role. Disillusioned learners have some level of competence, but they lack confidence or enthusiasm.

Similar to the employees who need to vent, these employees have lost some of their motivation. They started strong after onboarding but can't seem to turn the corner toward truly succeeding. The challenges they are facing feel enormous. Tasks that used to feel challenging and exciting now frustrate these employees. They are improving, but they feel discouraged by how slow their progress is. Even if your goals are realistic, they may

SUPPORTIVE FEEDBACK

begin to feel like they made a mistake or are not cut out for their role. By listening to these employees, you can identify where they are feeling the most discouragement and speak into that area. Remind them why they were hired and why success is important to them!

I frequently used this approach when leading first-time salespeople. Whenever I had to give feedback, I would share some of my personal experiences in the same area. When I started sales, I wasn't very effective. I was a good service driver and even made some upsells during my time in that role. But sales was not as easy of a transition as I had hoped. I was tempted to return to the service role, but my boss wouldn't let me. Sean assured me that what I felt was normal and that every salesperson has a learning curve. He committed to working with me as much as I wanted, to help me improve. He role-played cold calls with me, observed me on sales calls, and talked through my approach to the sales cycle. I wasn't immediately successful, but with his help, I achieved my goals and made President's Club! Just like he was there for me, I wanted to assure the people I led that I would be there for them too.

A more aggressive leader may have skipped over supportive feedback. Leaders who have an aggressive feedback style usually do not think that emotions have a place in the office. You are there to do a job and get paid. They will say things like, "Keep your personal problems out of the office!" They are much more likely to give directive feedback and point out an employee's failures than they are to ask questions and seek to understand.

These attitudes lead to distrust in the workplace. If you tell your employees you care about their personal and professional goals but fail to support them when they are struggling, they will believe that you are only concerned with their professional output. In the long term, they will look for employers who prove that they care about their employees. Feeling supported personally and professionally is especially important for Gen Z and millennials when they consider a new job opportunity. If you fail to provide supportive feedback, you can be sure that they will leave for another job whenever they get the chance.

When Not to Use Supportive Feedback

Of course, you cannot give empathetic feedback indefinitely. You will reach a point where you have done everything in your power to help your employee remove obstacles or overcome whatever personal or professional challenge they are facing. At this point, you will have to start injecting directive feedback into your conversations.

I once worked with a sales representative named Carrie. She was never late to a meeting, and she was highly coachable. The only problem was that she was not

SUPPORTIVE FEEDBACK

very good at sales. Week after week, we met to discuss her numbers. I gave her feedback and role-played scenarios with her. She promised to practice what she learned. The conversations looked like they were going well. I never saw anyone try as hard as Carrie did to succeed.

At first, I continued to give supportive feedback. I encouraged her to keep doing what she knew to do. You can be bad at sales and still succeed if you put in enough effort. I told her that she was doing all the right things and, eventually, she would start to see results.

But her numbers never improved. I was forced to start the disciplinary process. After the second write-up, I couldn't keep my focus on empathy. She needed to know the reality of the situation.

"Carrie, this is your second write-up for missing your numbers," I said. "If you get four write-ups, you will no longer be a part of the team."

She started to cry.

It was as though she did not fully understand the potential consequences of failing to meet her goals, even though it was clearly laid out in our handbook.

Giving her this feedback was important as it allowed her to prepare for what could happen. It made the consequences of failure much more real than if I had continued to give supportive feedback alone. It would have been unfair to continue to offer Carrie support without also being honest about where she was heading.

Leaders who naturally gravitate toward passive feedback are more likely to overuse supportive feedback. They want to avoid conflict and protect the way their employees view them. When approaching an underperformer, they see it as a way to ease into providing feedback in the hope that their kindness will compel the employee to meet their standard. This approach may work temporarily but fails to address underlying performance issues.

Employees who work under leaders who default to supportive feedback will learn that they can get out of accountability if they have a compelling, emotional reason. Supportive feedback should not allow your employees to avoid accountability. If their situation leads you to modify an expectation for a period of time, the goal is always to return to the full expectations for their role.

This is exactly the approach I take when my employees are dealing with a family emergency. I have experienced loss in my life, and I understand that your family comes first in those moments. It's okay if work does not have your full attention. I have been known to relax deadlines when appropriate and hold off on giving employees new projects while they are adjusting or grieving. Providing work-from-home opportunities, flexible hours, or modified workloads may be appropriate, depending on your situation.

Getting your employees past supportive feedback will help them fulfill their role in your company and continue moving toward their personal goals. When Sean gave me feedback on my performance, he balanced all three kinds of feedback. He started out with a lot of supportive feedback, then moved to directive and collaborative.

Let People Borrow Your Belief in Them

Supportive feedback is also a valuable tool for any mentor. As a leadership coach, I work with a number of executives, including Kevin, the CEO of a successful company. In one of our one-on-one sessions, Kevin admitted that he had missed his projections for the year. "This is the first time this has ever happened," he said. I have worked with Kevin for years, and I saw the pain and frustration on his face. I knew he had likely already heard an earful from his shareholders and employees. This failure was taking a toll on him, and he was not giving himself any excuses.

Kevin is an excellent person and a great leader. He didn't need me to go back to the leadership basics and drill him on what he could have done better. He didn't need a talking-to or a reminder about how many people were counting on him. He needed support! We spent a good portion of that meeting discussing how he felt about what was going on. I empathized and shared some of my own failures.

We eventually talked about some strategies he could take as a salesperson and leader, but the most beneficial part of the coaching wasn't the advice I gave. The goal was to show Kevin that he had a foundation of success and to let him borrow the confidence that I had in him. I knew that he could turn it around and meet his goals next year, but he needed that meeting so he could believe it for himself.

Supportive feedback allows you to take the posture of the voice of reason. It isn't the most glamorous style of feedback. In fact, you will probably talk less using this feedback than any other type.

That's what made Dr. Bradley such an effective leader. He gave great advice, yes, but he was a master of active listening. He let me, a zealous young leader, vent all of my frustrations. I was especially passionate about the church's youth ministry and responded aggressively when someone tried to argue against what we wanted to do. Afterward, Dr. Bradley let me call him and hear me vent about how I felt about the decisions that were made.

But once I stopped talking, Dr. Bradley, in his empathetic way, showed me how to do things differently. He acknowledged my excitement and my love for people but provided valuable feedback on how I could channel those

SUPPORTIVE FEEDBACK

characteristics in a way that furthered my cause. Over time, he helped me develop the confidence to present my ideas calmly and engage in professional discourse on the board. His guidance made me a better board member, a better leader, and a better man.

Dr. Bradley had a great influence on me, and I will value the time we spent on that board together for the rest of my life. He showed me just how powerful a mentor can be in helping you achieve your goals. Of course, we were both invested in my success as a board member, but he knew that mentoring me transcended church politics. He helped me find my footing as a leader and was one of the people who inspired me to keep pursuing leadership by demonstrating just how big of an impact one person can have.

Leaders must grasp all the types of feedback so that they can utilize each approach in the relevant situations. While Dr. Bradley's approach was largely supportive, he was not afraid to provide directive feedback when I needed it or to show me how to use collaborative feedback with other board members. These types of feedback are not stand-alone options or multiple-choice answers on a leadership test. They are part of a cohesive plan for leadership that requires an understanding of each employee's skills and personality. The best leaders don't just choose one and hope it works—they learn how to balance each type for each person.

Reflection Questions

Have you ever received supportive feedback? How did this approach make you feel? How did it affect your job performance?

What situations do you think call for supportive feedback? Are there any situations where supportive feedback is an unacceptable approach? Why or why not?

Application Activities

The best way to get good at supportive feedback is to become better at showing empathy. Empathy starts with curiosity. The more curious you are about how your employees are doing, the more you will take time to ask questions and listen carefully to their responses. Many employees fear looking weak or bothering their employer with their problems. In your weekly one-on-one meetings, make sure that you ask a few questions to better understand your employee's emotional state and identify any situations that may be affecting their ability to do their job. The more questions you ask, the more opportunities you will find to give supportive feedback.

SUPPORTIVE FEEDBACK

Supportive feedback requires employees to feel like they can be open and transparent with their boss. How have you built a culture of vulnerability among your team? One way to create a culture where people are willing to share what they are going through is by sharing some of your own struggles. You can be vulnerable by sharing a time when you struggled at work or home in the past or naming how current pressures are affecting you. The next time your team is facing a major challenge, find a way to encourage vulnerability. Vulnerability will allow you to truly assess how your team is doing and respond appropriately.

CHAPTER 10

Providing Accountability

The Backbone of Leadership

A re you Jeff Hancher?"

I was sitting outside a café and had just wrapped up a conference call with the other sales directors I worked with when a woman approached me.

"Yes," I said, quickly racking my brain, trying to remember where I knew her from. Had she worked with me in the past? Did we meet at church?

"My name is Jenna," she said. "It's so good to meet you. I listen to your podcast all the time!"

"Thanks!" I said. "What has stood out to you most?"

She went on to describe how an episode I released on the topic of feedback had challenged her mindset. "Honestly, I'm not very good at giving feedback, but I want to learn. Do you offer coaching, by chance?"

FIRM FEEDBACK IN A FRAGILE WORLD

At the time, I hadn't yet launched my own business, but I was excited by the opportunity to help another leader improve at giving feedback. "Absolutely," I said, deciding I would figure it out as I went along. "Here's my number. Reach out to me, and we'll set something up."

When Jenna and I met, she told me her whole story. She had been running a small business with six employees for years and never really figured out how to give great feedback. She had a passive approach and preferred to lead by cheering on her team and providing lots of encouragement.

"I know my approach isn't working. I'm seeing all the negative effects of the lack of feedback you talked about in your show. They're disengaged, they're missing important deadlines, and I'm so frustrated."

"What do you do when you get frustrated?" I asked.

"I try to keep it in, but eventually, I get to a boiling point where I explode. Last time it happened, I had an employee quit."

I nodded. I had seen many leaders go through the same thing, both from my employees and my bosses. Yet I could tell that she was passionate about her work and wanted to make a difference for her customers and her employees.

"Jenna," I said, "you have a great opportunity here, but it's not going to be easy. Are you ready?"

PROVIDING ACCOUNTABILITY

Expectations and Follow-Through

First, Jenna and I reviewed how to properly set expectations and earn the right to give feedback. We discussed the types of feedback and when to use them. Then I showed Jenna how to deliver this information to her team. After all, if sales taught me anything it is that the best way to handle an objection is with a great presentation.

When Jenna delivered this information to her team, they thought she was nuts. They thought she had undergone a full personality change. Their belief that she was nuts was only confirmed when she actually started holding people accountable!

The fact is that without follow-through, you may as well not set any expectations at all. Following through on addressing missed deadlines, errors, bad attitudes, and lateness (to name a few) is the key to getting the results you want. You can tell people that the expectation is for them to arrive on time, but if you never address employees when they arrive late, they will learn that your expectation is merely a good idea. It's not something you're willing to fight for—it's just something you hope will happen.

Leaders often become even more unwilling to address behavior the longer it happens.

It's one thing to talk to an employee and tell them that they were ten minutes late to the meeting. It's another to say that you have recognized a pattern of lateness and that this will be their first written warning.

Every time you don't address a missed expectation, you lose credibility. If you don't plan on holding people accountable, you may as well stop reading this book. None of the techniques will work if you use them inconsistently. You must commit to the expectations, hold yourself to them, and compassionately hold your team to them.

> *By choosing the appropriate feedback technique, you can meet the employee where they are and help them get back on track without looking heartless.*

Some leaders try to avoid accountability because they want to protect their employees. They rightly understand that many problems can cause employees to struggle to meet expectations. By choosing the appropriate feedback technique, you can meet the employee where they are and help them get back on track without looking heartless. However, if the problem continues and you have offered as much support as you can, it is time to move into accountability.

I recommend two key techniques when holding people accountable. Again, this process usually happens after you have already given directive, cooperative, and/or supportive feedback.

PROVIDING ACCOUNTABILITY

The Five Questions Technique

I have used this technique many times when addressing unmet expectations with service drivers, salespeople, managers, and volunteers. Asking questions ensures that you and your team members are speaking the same language and creates opportunities for clarification. One area I was committed to enforcing strictly was my company's policy on lifting and loading correctly. Because of the back injury I sustained, I never wanted any of my employees to go through the fear, pain, and stress that I endured as a result.

One day, I was walking down to the loading docks and saw an employee, Peter, loading a truck incorrectly. Immediately, I called him over and asked him to walk with me. We walked to a more private location. I explained that I'd seen him loading the box without bending his knees and started asking him these five questions:

1. Do you know what the expectation is?
2. Can you tell me what the expectation is?
3. Can you tell me why meeting or exceeding the expectation is good for you?
4. What behaviors will you change in the future to ensure that you meet or exceed the expectation?
5. If this behavior continues, what do you think we should do about it?

Do you know what the expectation is?

You want to first determine whether your employee is choosing not to meet the expectation or if they are trying and simply don't have the skills or support necessary. If an employee says they don't know the expectation, then you as the leader have missed an opportunity to make sure the expectation is clear. If an employee says they do know the expectation, then their actions reveal that they are choosing to believe that the expectation is unimportant. People believe expectations are unimportant for a variety of reasons. I call this the difference between a "can't do" and a "won't do." When an employee can't do a specific task, they fail because they don't have an awareness of the expectation or the training or resources necessary to fulfill it. When an employee won't do a particular task, it's because they have chosen to ignore the expectation. A can't do falls on the leader, but a won't do identifies a problem with the employee.

You have to be careful to identify the difference. When an employee is faced with a personal issue, they may be less effective. You might be tempted to criticize them and say that their ineffectiveness is a result of laziness or a lack of care. However, I have found that employees facing personal struggles often "can't" have the same level of success. Something in their life or work situation is causing them to be unable to meet the

PROVIDING ACCOUNTABILITY

expectations they normally do not struggle with. Identifying the difference will ensure you choose the correct approach. When an employee "won't do" what is asked, you must begin the accountability process. If you identify the issue as a "can't do," some understanding and coaching toward a gradual return to normalcy is the best course of action.

When I asked Peter if he knew what the expectation was around loading the boxes correctly, he nodded. Of course. Immediately I knew that Peter was able to fulfill the expectation I had set. If he wasn't following the company's guidelines, it was not because he couldn't. He had the physical strength, training, and awareness necessary to complete the task, but he chose to ignore those standards. I knew from experience that most service drivers will cut corners in proper lifting and loading procedures to save time and get done with their route faster. In this case, his failure to load the truck correctly was a "won't do."

Can you tell me what the expectation is?

You want to validate that you and your employee are on the same page about the expectation. If they say they understand but are unable to explain the expectation to you, there could be a communication issue. It's very common, especially with more complex tasks, for an employee to misunderstand the expectation. Gaining this understanding before you proceed is crucial.

Remember that having clear expectations is one way that you earn the right to hold someone accountable. If they cannot explain the expectation, you have not earned the right to hold them accountable!

When I asked Peter to explain the expectation to me, he was able to cite the exact procedure we teach over and over. I affirmed that his explanation was correct.

Can you tell me why meeting or exceeding the expectation is good for you?

This is where many leaders will start to make a mistake. After you learn that an employee is choosing not to meet your expectation or is trying to make excuses about their behavior, it's tempting to start to lay into them and lecture them on why they need to meet the expectation: The whole team is counting on you! You're creating problems for our customers. You could really hurt yourself. If this continues, you could get fired. Do you really want that?

For a person who is feeling defensive or cornered, doubling down on why you think it is important for them to meet your expectation will be counterproductive. Their work is not about you or your numbers, quota, or reputation. It's about the employee! Keep the conversation on their potential and value.

PROVIDING ACCOUNTABILITY

Remember when you set goals with your employee and found out why success is important to them? Go back to that discussion and re-create buy-in. Often, an employee who is choosing not to follow proper procedures has become disconnected from their goals. Asking your employee this question allows them to take the lead, but if they need some help coming up with a good answer, you can nudge them in the right direction by reminding them of their goals.

As we started talking about why the expectation was important to him, Peter cited my experience. "I remember you telling me your story during my orientation. I remember you saying how scared you were and how it impacted you and your family. It scared me a little, to be honest. I mean, I have a wife at home too. She would be so scared if I got hurt, especially if I couldn't work anymore. I guess I need to follow the expectation so that doesn't happen to me or my family."

Telling an employee why they should meet your expectation will only get you compliance. By encouraging your employee to tell you why it is important, you are allowing them to take ownership of their future progress. Next time they are faced with the choice to meet the expectation or not, they will think back to what they said. Instead of obeying you because they are afraid of punishment, they will engage with why they decided the expectation was important.

What behaviors will you change in the future to ensure that you meet or exceed the expectation?

You may think you know exactly what your employee will need to change to meet your expectations. Don't tell them the answer! You're not withholding this information from them to be cruel. You're allowing them to come up with their own answer that they think will work. Again, remember that your employee is likely feeling nervous and defensive. No one wants to be held accountable by their boss. Everyone knows that an accountability conversation could become a discussion about the possibility of termination if it goes badly. This employee does not need you to scold them. They need you to collaborate with them. If you ask this question and give them the answer, you're utilizing directive feedback. Asking this question gives you the opportunity to use collaborative feedback and have them be a part of the solution.

"To be honest," he said, "I was just in a rush. I'm really hoping to get home on time tonight, Jeff. My kid has a baseball game and my wife could really use my help getting everyone ready. But I know that wasn't safe."

"So you were in a rush to get home to your family," I said, summarizing what he said.

PROVIDING ACCOUNTABILITY

"Yeah. I don't know. I guess I could get someone to help me or come in a little earlier next time I need to be somewhere after work."

Ideally, your employee will come up with a great plan to ensure their future success. But in the event that they give a response that is unlikely to result in them meeting or exceeding your expectation, use the collaborative approach to nudge them in the right direction. Remember, the whole goal here is to get them communicating so it is their plan, not yours.

If this behavior continues, what do you think we should do about it?

This is accountability. This is where the rubber meets the road. Many leaders will list the consequences here. The fact is, your employees already know the consequences. At this point in the conversation, you've already established that they know the expectation and were properly trained. Here, you're trying to get buy-in on what will happen if the behavior continues. If three weeks later you have to talk to Peter about lifting the box incorrectly again, he already knows what to expect. By asking this final question, you make future tough conversations on the same issue much easier to navigate.

When I asked Peter this question, he said, "I guess I'd get written up. Or maybe I'd have to do that training again?"

"I think both of those are possible, yes," I said. "I just want to see you doing your job safely. I hope you know that."

"Yeah, I know."

"Do you have any questions? Is there anything I can do for you?"

"No, I don't think so. I just want to get back to my route now."

"Go for it. Have a good day, Peter!" I clapped him on the shoulder and sent him on his way.

Notice that throughout this conversation, I didn't say much. I established what I saw, asked questions, engaged in active listening, and provided some support at the end. Using the questions is a great way to get used to mining this information, but don't be afraid to ask them in a way that feels natural for you and your team as you get more comfortable.

After one of my workshops, a team member came up to me and asked, "Have you used these questions with me?" I affirmed that yes, I had.

"I figured," she said, "but I don't remember you asking the questions. It didn't feel like accountability—it just felt like a normal conversation."

As you get more comfortable with this approach, you can use your own questions to get the information you need from your employees. First, establish whether you're dealing with a "can't do" or "won't do," validate the expectation, justify the value of the expectation, gain buy-in, and set the stage for accountability.

Situation Behavior Impact Intent (SBII) Technique

Situation Behavior Impact Intent (SBII) was developed by the Center for Creative Leadership. The SBII technique can be used to address unmet expectations, but it is especially helpful when dealing with disruptive behavior.

Consider Brian. Brian manages a staff of marketers. In a team meeting to discuss the approach for an upcoming project, Brian's employee Eric seems frustrated. Eric is distant and is not participating in the discussion. Finally, when Eric speaks, he interrupts Brian by saying, "Why do you think your stupid idea is going to work this time? It didn't work last time, and I'm not going to do it your way again."

Brian is stunned. He's feeling upset that Eric disrespected him in front of the team, and now he has to figure out how to handle Eric's outburst and keep the team on track. He knows that the way he responds will show the rest of the team whether he will tolerate this behavior.

FIRM FEEDBACK IN A FRAGILE WORLD

What should Brian do?

A leader who naturally leans toward aggressive feedback will follow their instinct to directly address the employee right away. They'll say things like, "No one on this team is going to talk to me like that." They don't want the rest of the team to think that they're weak or that they will allow anyone to publicly disrespect them. However, the goal of feedback in these situations is to restore the relationship.

Providing great feedback and accountability takes time. Doing it publicly will result in an abridged conversation and will likely cause your employee to be untruthful or closed off just to get through the conversation and back to the meeting.

The key here is to address the need for feedback in the meeting and then follow up immediately after. Brian chooses to stay composed, thanks Eric for his feedback and says, "At the conclusion of this meeting, you and I will have a private meeting to discuss your thoughts, and I will provide mine as well." By publicly setting up the follow-up, you ensure that your team knows you are addressing the issue, but you protect the employee from being held accountable in front of their peers. Then, you can use the SBII technique to address the issue privately and restore your relationship with the employee and their relationship with the rest of the team.

PROVIDING ACCOUNTABILITY

Let's go a little bit deeper by taking a look at each aspect of SBII.

Situation

When Brian meets with Eric, the first thing he should do is describe the situation in which the behavior occurred. Ideally, you will be able to give prompt feedback, but if you must wait to have a conversation, describing the situation will ensure you and your employee are on the same page. You will also avoid making accusations or generalities that may or may not be accurate. Brian should start his meeting by saying, "In the 10 a.m. marketing meeting . . ."

Behavior

Next, Brian should describe the behavior without emotion or exaggeration. Remember, feedback is data! Focus on what happened and any relevant information to support your claim. Avoid using generalizations or attacking the person. You never want to use feedback as an opportunity to label your employees as "always disrespectful," "never considerate," or "self-absorbed." To properly describe what happened, Brian should say, "You interrupted me in the middle of my presentation." Notice that this feedback is not emotional or subjective—it is just data.

Impact

Then, Brian will need to describe the impact of the behavior. Again, the goal is not to pass judgment. Instead, describe how the behavior made you or others feel and how it affected the work you were trying to accomplish. The listener is more likely to absorb what you're saying when you focus on the facts. An impact of their behavior could be anything from interrupting the workday and causing delayed results to making someone on the team cry. In this situation, Brian would say, "I felt disrespected, and your comments made the team seem worried and uncomfortable. No one spoke up after you interrupted me and we did not accomplish our meeting objectives."

Additionally, you can tie the impact of the situation to how it affects the employee's goals. If Eric wants to be promoted someday, Brian can address how his behavior would negatively affect the likelihood that he will be considered for a leadership position.

This piece is especially important because it clarifies why the behavior you're addressing matters. Humans are naturally self-absorbed. When you're frustrated or in a rush, you're usually not thinking about how others feel.

PROVIDING ACCOUNTABILITY

Just think of any time someone has beeped at you in traffic for not going fast enough! People are always on the lookout for what is best for them in the moment.

By describing the impact, you are taking the focus off the behavior and onto the team and processes the behavior impacted. This is much more powerful than merely being told that obedience to company policies is mandatory; it gets your employees to buy into the vision of the behavior you want them to do.

Intent

The last piece of this technique requires Brian to ask what Eric was trying to accomplish with his behavior. In other words, what was his intent? When people act out, they are usually doing so for a reason. Maybe they felt misunderstood or frustrated and that no one was listening to them. Asking about intent turns what could be very directive feedback into an opportunity for collaboration and support.

When Eric arrived in Brian's office, Brian started by describing the situation and behavior:

"Eric, in the 10 a.m. marketing meeting to discuss our strategy for our new client, you interrupted me. I felt really disrespected by what you said, and the rest of the team seemed uncomfortable and worried. No one spoke up voluntarily after you interrupted me, and as a result, we did not accomplish our meeting objectives. Also, I know you want to be promoted someday, but when you interrupt meetings like that, it really hurts your credibility with the team. Help me understand. What were you hoping to accomplish when you interrupted me?"

By using this approach, Brian provided clarity to his expectation and invited Eric to be a part of coming up with a solution. From here, Eric has the opportunity to clarify how he was feeling, why he interrupted, and what he needs in order to feel more satisfied with the approach the team is taking. After Eric responds, Brian can choose how to proceed based on this response. If he is apologetic and opens up about what he was thinking, Brian could choose a collaborative approach and coach Eric on how to better present his ideas. If Eric is feeling overwhelmed by the new project, Brian could help Eric identify where he needs support or additional clarity. If Eric continues to speak disrespectfully, Brian also has the opportunity to start the disciplinary process.

The best part about this approach is that it allows the leader to flow into whatever feedback technique they want to use next.

The Consequences of Accountability

Most people feel uneasy giving feedback, let alone holding someone accountable. That's why I always

PROVIDING ACCOUNTABILITY

role-play accountability situations with my coaching clients, to help them feel more comfortable.

When I started working with Jenna, we role-played every feedback and accountability conversation.

Here's what happened when she started holding people accountable:

Fifty percent of her team quit in the first few months.

Luckily, I had warned her about this. Any time leaders start applying a new leadership strategy and begin doing something they have never done before, people quit. It's not because suddenly the leader isn't a nice person. They quit because they didn't sign up for that leadership style. Ultimately, the culture and values of the organization changed, and they were no longer a good fit.

You might be shaking in your boots and thinking about putting this book back on the shelf. Losing fifty percent of my workforce? No thanks!

Before you give up, I want you to answer the same question I asked Jenna when she raised the same objection:

What if you don't hold them accountable?

What if you allow your team to continue to meet your expectations only when they feel like it or when it is convenient for them?

I explained to Jenna that while there is a temporary cost to accountability, she will do long-term damage to her company if she continues on her current path. She will continue to get frustrated and blow up on her team. She will keep having employees who make frequent errors and are disengaged from the goals they are working toward. Over time, people will quit, productivity will fall, and eventually, her company will not exist.

After the initial wave of resignations, Jenna was able to hire people who were aligned with the culture she was creating. Today, her employees don't just accept feedback—they look for feedback. They crave it! Her team understands that feedback is what makes them better and allows them to reach their professional and personal goals. Her retention statistics are amazing now, and she continues to grow her company beyond where it was when we first met.

I'm so thankful that Jenna noticed me working outside that summer day and was bold enough to ask for help. Many leaders struggle to grow because they don't have the self-awareness to notice their weaknesses, seek out feedback, and hold themselves accountable. Often, they are the very thing standing in the way of their success. If you're ready to grow your team and create a culture where feedback and accountability are the norm, you must find ways to not only hold others accountable but also hold yourself accountable.

PROVIDING ACCOUNTABILITY

Reflection Questions

When you think about holding people on your team account-able, how do you feel? How have people responded in the past when you tried to hold them accountable?

What do you think will happen if you don't hold people accountable? What are the results for the company? What are the results for the employees? What positive results could you achieve if you started holding people account-able more?

Application Activity

Role-play these techniques with a mentor or peer. Pick a few situations that happen frequently at your company and take turns being the boss and employee. How do you feel while asking the questions? How do you feel while answering the questions? What other situations could you use these tech-niques to address?

--- CHAPTER 11 ---

Eliminating Blind Spots

How Leaders Can Grow Their Feedback Skills

You can grow only if you find people willing to give you feedback.

When I was on my church's board, Dr. Bradley was one board member who stood above the rest and was willing to take me under his wing. I've always been driven and direct. When I see something I believe in, I am willing to fight for it. That tenacity does not get you votes in a board meeting, though.

After every meeting, Dr. Bradley would let me vent about what frustrated me, and then he would start to dissect my approach. He pointed out every time I became argumentative or raised my voice; he began to coach me on staying calm while getting my point across. He also helped me realize that I don't have to die on every hill—that you can create more change by focusing on the battles that matter most to you.

Without such a mentor, I don't think I would have made a very good board member. His insight and ability to help me see my blind spots made me a better leader and a better man.

Every leader needs someone like him to help them grow, but most leaders don't have someone like Dr. Bradley. Most employees find it hard to give feedback to the person who can influence whether they get a raise or promotion.

The problem is that leaders are especially vulnerable to blind spots because no one wants to upset their boss. People tend to withhold feedback when they feel like the perceived risk is greater than the potential reward. As much as you need to learn the art of giving feedback, leaders must be equally skilled at soliciting and receiving feedback. The more feedback you receive, the better feedback you will give.

So, what can you do to ensure you are getting the feedback you need to lead your team well?

Cultivate Personal Reflective Practices

Personal reflective practices are a crucial part of personal growth. Regularly evaluating your actions is an excellent

ELIMINATING BLIND SPOTS

way to determine where you need to grow as a leader. However, you have to be willing to be honest with yourself. Psychologists describe the "self-serving bias" as our tendency to attribute our negative attitudes and behaviors to external factors. We blame our outburst during the team meeting on the stubbornness of the other leaders or the fact that the coffee line was too long and we didn't have time to get our morning latte.

Of course, while those factors may have contributed to your failure, your actions are your responsibility. Time is a scarce commodity for leaders, but you must block out time for self-reflection. You cannot afford to allow your bad habits or impulsive behaviors to ruin your reputation as a leader. People are counting on you to set the standard for patience, accountability, and composure.

Self-reflection allows you to identify the areas you want to improve. For me, this area is calling out what people are doing well. As much as I preach using feedback to reinforce the good work people are doing, I know it is a natural weakness of mine. I can get so focused on the results that I forget to outwardly appreciate the people who make the results possible. To avoid this mistake, I seek out feedback and pay close attention to how the people around me are responding to my leadership.

For this reason, I resisted having my wife employed with my business for a long time. My direct and, at times, harsh approach to feedback was something I had to work hard on early in our marriage. It took a lot of openness and vulnerability to talk through how my communication affected her and what she needed from me to feel safe and cared for. We have made a lot of progress and have a wonderful marriage. I hesitated to invite unnecessary conflict by also hiring her as an employee.

The problem with working with someone you know well is that it becomes very easy to take them for granted and act too familiar. Familiarity is the reason you might say things to your spouse, children, or parents that you would never say to a stranger on the street. They get you. They know the challenges you are facing and the bad habits you have. They're much more likely to give you grace and forgive you than a random stranger that you've worked with for a month or two. The problem is that because of your relationship, you may not realize how your actions negatively affect them until it is too late.

However, a few years into running my own company, I realized that I needed help, and my wife's talents were a great fit. Besides, she already was traveling with me to my workshops and speaking engagements whenever she could. Hiring her was the natural next step. We talked up front about expectations, and I warned her that I would be inclined to be more direct and tough on her than I am on anyone else. I didn't say all of that to excuse any bad behavior on my part. I said it so we could set the expectation that if something came up, she could feel comfortable addressing it with me. While she has pointed out times when I have fallen short in this area, I know that I will be a better leader if I can identify those missteps and make corrections before they become problems.

Every day, I evaluate the way I treat my employees, especially my wife. It doesn't have to take long. I go over our interactions in my mind and ask myself these questions:

Did I give feedback in a way my employees could receive?

Did I respond emotionally instead of responding from a place of understanding and curiosity?

Did I intentionally make deposits into my team today?

Did I find people doing things right?

Did I push forward in a conversation instead of responding to my employee's cues?

These questions help me stay on top of my tendencies so that I can be the leader I want to be for my employees. I have been doing this long enough that I usually don't identify many mistakes, but when I do, I make the effort to reach out and correct my errors.

Building a self-reflective practice will help you identify your errors before your employees start to see them as a pattern. This practice is even more effective when you have other avenues for feedback from your team, boss, and peers. But how do you get people to give you feedback?

Ask for Feedback

The best way to get feedback is to ask for it. Give your employees the safety of knowing that they aren't going to blindside you. Show them that you want to hear what they have to say and that you trust their opinions.

The only problem with this approach is that people might hesitate to be honest because they fear retaliation. Even in an "anonymous" survey, employees who do not have high trust in their leadership will give false, overly positive responses.

Because of this, leaders must work extra hard to cultivate their relationships and ensure their team feels safe talking to them about anything. If you want to create a culture of feedback, you must set the tone. The more deposits you make into your team, the more you will be able to ask them. If you can continually show them that you are open and vulnerable, you can prove that you are genuinely interested in becoming a better leader.

Do not ask for feedback in person if you are unprepared to take the high road and admit you were wrong. If you create a track record as someone who will get defensive when given feedback, your team will not feel safe

ELIMINATING BLIND SPOTS

enough to give you feedback even when you ask. Know your own tendencies and mentally prepare before you ask for feedback. For example, I know that I can come off as defensive and even aggressive if I receive feedback I don't understand or agree with. Before meeting with employees, I make the conscious decision to be empathetic and curious. If someone is willing to be vulnerable enough to give me feedback, I want to show them I value it.

You can also create trust by sharing times when other people have pointed out something you've done wrong. Your employees will see that giving you feedback will not result in being ostracized or overlooked for new opportunities. You will take their feedback, evaluate it, and make any necessary modifications.

When you have your team's trust, you can create systems to hear more feedback. I always recommend that companies conduct regular surveys to assess the temperature of their team and organization as a whole. While yearly company-wide surveys can offer excellent insights, offering surveys on, say, an employee's employment anniversary can help you get staggered feedback and identify blind spots more quickly.

Asking for feedback during your one-on-one meetings with employees will also help ensure you are staying on top of potential problems or bad habits in your leadership. Simple questions like, "What's something I should stop doing as a leader?" "Where did I drop the ball this year?" or "What can I be doing to lead you better?" can give your employees the freedom to speak up. The more they feel like you appreciate their feedback, the more likely they are to offer you feedback in the future. Focus on getting a complete understanding of what they experienced, the role you played, and what you could do differently next time.

You know that you are doing this well when your employees willingly offer you feedback without you asking. During one meeting with an employee, she asked if she could talk to me about something. I said yes and quickly made sure I was ready to listen to her and ask great questions.

She started to recount a situation that happened over a month earlier over Thanksgiving. I had noticed that she missed some deadlines over the break. Instead of calling her, I sent her an email about the error. She apologized and made the necessary corrections. We have a good working relationship, and she usually takes feedback from me well, so I thought we were fine.

"First of all, I know that I messed up, and I should have communicated better. But the email you sent made me feel really upset," she said.

Inside, I felt blindsided and defensive. It had been weeks since this interaction. But because I knew I could

ELIMINATING BLIND SPOTS

become defensive easily, I stayed silent and focused on listening to understand what she was feeling.

She cited what I said and clarified that she felt like I was focused on one mistake instead of how she had been going above and beyond the rest of the month. The way I worded my email made her feel like I didn't appreciate her, her job was at risk, and worse, that I thought she was uncommitted to our mission.

I did not want to make her feel that way at all. I appreciated her a lot! I was just trying to ensure we reached our goals and stayed on track. To be fair, I sent the email late at night, and I should have been more patient and given the feedback on the phone when I was less emotional. The feedback was true, but my delivery was inappropriate.

"Why did it take so long for you to tell me how you felt?" I asked.

"I didn't want to cry," she said, her voice breaking on the final word.

I've worked with this team member long enough to know that she cries easily, so I wasn't shaken at all.

"I'd rather you cry than keep something like this from me. I'm sorry my email came off that way. It was not my intention."

We talked through how we could both give and receive feedback better, and I assured her that I valued her feedback and didn't want her to keep anything like this from me. Clear, quick feedback is the best way to keep lines of communication open and prevent anyone from developing a false narrative. I can't help but think that this situation could have ended much differently if we had a different relationship. Instead of addressing the problem, she could have become resentful or even quit. But because we have a long history together and I have made many investments in her over the years, she felt safe enough to share her true feelings.

> *Clear, quick feedback is the best way to keep lines of communication open and prevent anyone from developing a false narrative.*

Another way you can get feedback at work is by asking for it from your boss. Your one-on-one meetings are a great opportunity to ask for feedback. If you do not have one-on-ones or they are infrequent, take the initiative to set up a meeting. Just like you prepare yourself to hear feedback from your team, prepare for the feedback you may get from your boss. If your boss is giving you feedback, ensure that you are responding appropriately. Remember, feedback is morally neutral. The information you receive will help you improve. Take it one step further by asking what resources, training, or mentorships the company could offer to help you improve.

ELIMINATING BLIND SPOTS

Join a Mastermind Group

Over the last few years, I have become especially passionate about the value of mastermind groups in helping senior leaders receive feedback. I started running a mastermind in 2020 when many leaders were facing an onslaught of challenges, both professional and personal. We meet virtually to discuss the issues we are facing and then open the floor to advice, suggestions, or personal experiences. Many of the leaders on this call are upper-level managers, entrepreneurs, or CEOs. The best part of the mastermind is that I do not have to come up with perfect answers for every person. There is so much experience in the room that there is always someone who has gone through something similar and can share what they went through and whether their approach worked or not.

Recently, our mastermind has been navigating many conversations around remote work and whether they should start requiring more time in the office. One of my coaching clients who is in the group worked with his executive team to create a plan to move employees back to the office. When he rolled out the plan, he immediately saw 25 percent of his employees resign! We spent our monthly meeting talking about what he could have done differently and how he could help his company get

FIRM FEEDBACK IN A FRAGILE WORLD

on board with the changes. But he also brought it up at our mastermind's next in-person session.

He explained the challenge he was having, how it came about, and what he was trying to do to fix it. Other leaders started to hear similar stories from around the room. They shared times they also struggled to get employees to be excited about change and what helped them. The more people talked, the more he realized that he had been viewing the change from his perspective as a leader and less from the perspective of his employees. He had been working through the challenges of returning to the office for months, so he had already processed many of his feelings toward the idea with senior leaders. This change was brand-new to his employees, and they were likely responding to those feelings of loss.

We talked through ways he could help prepare his employees for any future changes. Other leaders shared what had worked for them and the mistakes they made along the way. By hearing feedback from his peers, he got better support than he could have from talking to me alone. Groups like masterminds are great at connecting people and helping leaders get honest feedback and turn that feedback into action.

You cannot expect to succeed as a leader on your own. If you don't have a community that can support you, find one. Leaders who choose to go it alone experience the silo effect. Silos, of course, are large buildings that store a specific type of product on a farm. In business, silos develop when we refuse to share or receive insight from other departments, mentors, and employees. Silos are effective for farms but disastrous for businesses.

When silos exist in businesses, they break down communication between departments and reduce the cohesiveness of the organization. Instead of being able to work together to solve problems, people are left trying to fill in the gaps on their own. They become ineffective, slow, and self-destructive. However, leaders often don't realize this until it's too late. Leaders buy into the idea that they have to have all the answers and that reaching out for help or accepting feedback from others will harm their reputation.

Leaders who are siloed are more likely to have harmful blind spots and make poor decisions. As uncomfortable as vulnerability can be, it is the key to a long and successful career. The more vulnerable you are, the more often you will receive feedback. Consider two bosses. Both know that they often fail to follow through on ideas their employees have suggested to improve their processes. One boss assures you that they will follow through and this time will be different, while the other acknowledges their tendency and asks you to follow up with them if they haven't reached out with next steps by the end of the week. One leader is siloed, trying to do everything on their own, and the other is open, vulnerable, and willing to ask for help.

Which leader would you rather work for?

Which leader will be more successful long term?

Which leader would make you more willing to respond to the feedback they gave you?

How you handle yourself as a leader will determine the respect you garner from your team. If you are open to growth and development, they will be more likely to do the same. The more you own up to your mistakes and show them that everyone makes mistakes occasionally, the more willing they will be to take ownership of their mistakes.

Ultimately, you are in charge of the feedback culture on your team. You get to decide whether yours will be a team that openly gives and receives feedback or a team that is individualistic and just hopes for the best.

Reflection Questions

Think about a time when you gave feedback to one of your managers or leaders. How did they respond? How did their response affect your willingness to give them feedback in the future?

ELIMINATING BLIND SPOTS

Describe a person in your life who is helping you improve. How did you get connected? What do you think you could do to give and receive even more in that relationship?

Application Activities

Reflective journaling can be a great way to get insight into how you respond to stressors and how to respond differently in the future. Set aside a few minutes at the end of every day to journal about the experiences you had. As you write, ask yourself how you responded, why you responded that way, and the impacts of your response. Then, journal about what you could do the next time a similar situation arises.

Develop a rhythm for asking for feedback. Regular meetings with a mentor or mastermind group are great ways to get feedback from people who are also going through the challenges of leadership. Asking for feedback from your team will give you real-time data on how you can be a better leader. When you ask for feedback, make sure that you use specific questions. The more specific, the more likely you are to get actionable feedback. Specific questions also build trust by proving that you are reflecting on your actions and are aware of areas where you may need to improve. For example:

- What could I have done to better support you while you were completing your latest project?
- Have you ever felt like I tried to micromanage your work?
- How did my comments in the latest team meeting come off? Is there anything I should have said differently?

--- CHAPTER 12 ---

Building Your Leadership Legacy
Making Feedback Your Gift to Others

Feedback is a gift.

I earned my first President's Club award thanks to Sean pulling me into his office after my mom died and giving me constant feedback on how to be a better salesperson. As part of the award, my wife and I were invited to the Broadmoor in Colorado Springs. I was excited for the awards dinner, but the environment was overwhelming. There were more pieces of silverware on my plate than I knew what to do with. I wore a borrowed sports coat and was beginning to feel like an imposter.

But as I sat, I started to reflect on the wild ride that had brought me to this moment. It began to sink in just how much I had overcome to get there. I thought about going to the welfare office with my dad and watching him fight for me and my brother. I thought about how I failed my first sales job interview and then nearly emptied my bank account to purchase the Dale Carnegie sales course.

The trip was an incredible reward, but I was celebrating so much more than just meeting a sales goal. I knew that even though my mom wasn't around anymore, I was making her proud. I was celebrating finding a way to get out of poverty and create a life I never dreamed was possible. I was celebrating a newfound confidence. I didn't have to be defined as the kid who grew up in poverty. I could write my own story.

This is just one of the many times my life was changed by a leader who cared enough to give me the gift of feedback. Whether it was Dr. Joe Bradley teaching me how to accomplish my goals without raising my voice, Sean pushing me to set new goals after my mom died, or Brad reminding me why feedback is important, I would not be where I am without their feedback.

If this book seems heavy on relationship building, that's because it is. Strong relationships with your employees are what prepare them to accept your feedback. Making big deposits allows you to make big withdrawals.

When I present this information, I'll always have someone complain that the approach sounds too soft: Why should you spend this much time trying to convince your employees to do their job? I received the same criticism when I worked in corporate America. My boss once told me I was too soft, to which I responded, "Have you asked my team if I'm too soft?"

Many of the people I have led will tell you that I am tough on them. I have high expectations, and I want to see you give your best. But if I can do that while also acknowledging, valuing, and supporting you as a person, I will earn your trust and respect. You can be hard on expectations while being soft on people.

This approach isn't limited to just one industry. I have seen CEOs and mid-level managers alike use healthy feedback in just about every business type, from sales to construction to nonprofits and more.

One of my first coaching clients was Rob, who was hired as the executive director of a charity that supports military veterans. I have partnered with this organization for years by hosting a fundraiser and am a huge supporter of their work. So, when Rob took on this new role, he called me to get my thoughts.

As a fellow veteran, I have seen some of my friends struggle with civilian life, so I was eager to hear about Rob's work. He had a lot of new ideas but was challenged with getting his team to pursue buy-in and embrace his perspective. As we talked about his new job, it became clear to me that he needed to create a culture where people would expect and welcome feedback.

FIRM FEEDBACK IN A FRAGILE WORLD

I started by helping Rob improve his own leadership by teaching him the principles in this book. Then, we set up a group training so his entire staff of leaders would be better equipped to give and receive feedback.

We gathered Rob's staff into a small conference room and began the training. An hour or so into the presentation, the majority of the attendees got up and quickly walked or ran out. I've seen a lot of unique behaviors at my trainings, but never anything of this magnitude. I can usually keep teaching through anything, but this was extreme. I looked to Rob, who suggested taking a break. As the remaining employees started talking to each other and leaving the room, Rob explained to me that the people who left had been called to a code red.

"What's a code red?" I asked.

"It means there's a veteran trying to take his life," Rob said. "I need to check in on this, but please don't leave. I'll be back as soon as I can."

An hour later Rob returned. I offered to reschedule since we had lost time due to the interruption. "I'm sure your team needs some time to regroup and process what just happened. It's no problem for me to come back another day."

"No, I think we need to continue," he said. "We just had a man hold a knife to his throat and threaten to kill himself. We literally had to wrestle the knife away from

BUILDING YOUR LEADERSHIP LEGACY

him. Thankfully he is still alive and is getting the help he needs, but I'll be honest, our team wasn't ready. We were slower than we should have been and nearly missed some crucial steps."

I nodded along.

"Jeff, I think you need to stay and talk about what just happened," he continued. "When we get things wrong or don't follow procedure, people die. We need to know how to give and receive feedback because the costs of getting it wrong in this line of work are just too high."

With Rob's blessing, we reassembled the team and started talking to them about why expectations were important. "You all just saw one of your goals first-hand," I said. "You exist to make sure that veterans get the support they need so they don't end up homeless or try to commit suicide, and if they do, you save their life. Rob tells me that's what you just did. Let me ask you this. Were you prepared? Did you know what the expectation for your role in that code red was? Did your employees know?"

I let the room sit with those questions for a minute and then added, "Let me follow up by asking you this: Did you execute your assignment? Did your team?

"I teach this to people who are selling uniforms and laundry services. I teach this to people selling first aid kits. But you and your employees are all on the front

FIRM FEEDBACK IN A FRAGILE WORLD

line. These veterans don't have anyone else to lean on. They're looking to you and the support you can offer to them. What happens if you fail?

"Today, the cost of failure could have been a person's life. Thank God it wasn't. Thank God he's okay. But what if he wasn't? What if you weren't prepared because you weren't adequately trained? Or worse, you just didn't do what you knew you should do? Expectations, feedback, and accountability are what help organizations thrive and grow and create unity. But for you guys, expectations, feedback, and accountability can be the difference between life and death. You may not like everything Rob wants to do. You may have questions or prefer the old way. But you have to be willing to put your preferences and pride aside and start not only accepting feedback but asking for it. It's that important."

We finished the training, which covered most of the material in this book, and I continued to meet with Rob. Over the next two years, he saw his team buy into the vision. The organization not only started meeting its goals but began exceeding them. They raised millions of dollars to build a new transitional housing program for homeless veterans and became the number one grantee through Pennsylvania's Department of Labor employment program. Neither of those had ever been done by this company! Why were they able to change? Because everyone bought into the value of feedback to see the organization fulfill its mission and vision.

A few years later, Rob was recruited to become the first director of the Department of Human Services in a county in Pennsylvania. He was tasked with bringing five distinct departments with a combined three hundred employees and a $300 million budget under the DHS umbrella. No one had done anything like this before, so Rob had to reimagine the way the government worked. The first time he brought me in to teach leadership training, the staff was still angry over the restructuring. But we painted the picture of the tens of thousands of lives that are impacted by this team's ability to do their jobs well.

I coached Rob on investing in each of the department heads, soliciting feedback, and setting clear expectations. Just two years later, the state government was calling him to find out how they could replicate his results in other counties across Pennsylvania!

The difference was in feedback. Instead of dreading feedback and fighting for their own departments, leaders started asking for feedback. They recognized how serious their work was, and they felt like their efforts were valued.

In both employment situations, Rob was able to set clear expectations, create buy-in, connect the organization's goals to the employee's goals, and engage in healthy accountability. Was it easy? No. His teams were in very

FIRM FEEDBACK IN A FRAGILE WORLD

fragile positions. They were being asked to change a lot about the way they did their jobs. But over time, as Rob continued to invest in them and clarify the vision, they came around. The culture at these organizations became one where people didn't just accept feedback—they craved it!

The moments when people get life-changing feedback are rarely the moments where they are exceeding expectations. Most of the time, feedback becomes necessary during the most fragile moments in our lives. It's big events like starting a new job, navigating a scary diagnosis, losing a parent, or facing financial challenges that disrupt the norm and create tension that spills into our work.

It's impossible to completely avoid tension. Everyone goes through challenges that make them feel like the world is crumbling around them. But when you have made deposits into your employees, set clear expectations, and committed yourself to helping them reach their goals, you have earned the right and the responsibility to give feedback. In peoples' darkest moments, feedback from a leader who cares for them isn't an attack—it's a gift.

I remember working with an employee who was just not good at his job. He was a hard worker, but no matter how hard he tried or how much I worked with him, he could not achieve his sales goals. As we reached our last few conversations before this employee was fired, I started spending extra time talking to him about what he wanted in life. We talked about his strengths and the kind of work that he enjoyed.

In peoples' darkest moments, feedback from a leader who cares for them isn't an attack—it's a gift.

"Ken," I explained, "if your performance doesn't change, you're not going to be on this team much longer. But I think you could be really successful in a job that is more focused on customer service. I would be happy to write a recommendation for you if you decide to go that direction."

Ken didn't want to leave the company, so he just kept doing what he knew to do. Eventually, I did have to fire Ken. It did not feel good. I liked Ken. He was a good employee, and I genuinely wanted the best for him. He went on to get a job at a different company and thrived where he could use his natural skill set.

A few years later, I got a call from Ken. My company had just hired him again! This time as a customer service representative. Ken was thrilled to be back with the company he enjoyed working for, and I was thrilled that through the pain of our conversations, Ken found a job that allowed him to embrace his strengths. Even though my feedback probably hurt in the moment, it created an opportunity for Ken to find a career that he could thrive in.

A Reward Worth Fighting For

This situation was tense at times. But leaders don't run away from tension. They lean into it. They embrace discomfort because it is worth fighting for their employees and their goals.

Can you imagine what your company could look like if your employees considered feedback a gift? What could your team accomplish? How could their individual lives change for the better? You don't have to be a genius or have a naturally magnetic personality. Any leader who applies these principles can create a culture where feedback is valued and creates stability rather than fragility.

Today, you may be leading a team of people who are just there to collect a paycheck. They have their own personal lives and problems. The common attitude is that if your job starts asking too much of you, just quit. Find a new job and a boss who will respect your boundaries. You may live with a real fear of losing people if you try to take this approach.

But that's why you must start with the relationship. Getting to know your people is the only way you can earn the right to give them feedback. The more deposits you can make into your employees, the more they will be willing (and even excited) to hear your feedback. Then, you're not a monster who is just pushing for results—you're a partner working to help them reach their goals. I've found that the employees who both believe in the vision of the company and feel genuinely cared for are the ones who will stick around the longest.

Once you have established the right to give feedback, you can start utilizing the feedback techniques in this book. These techniques are not designed to be a script but rather a way to approach feedback differently in different situations. Utilizing the right feedback technique will help ensure your feedback isn't misunderstood.

The more feedback you can give, the better. According to Gallup, employees who receive weekly feedback are four times more engaged than those who do not.[18] Frequent feedback gives you the opportunity to reinforce the things your team members do well and redirect them when they are not meeting your expectations. This means your employees can act confidently, knowing what you expect and whether or not they are meeting those expectations.

Finally, accountability is critically important. When you notice a pattern of unmet expectations or an employee doing something dangerous, immoral, or costly, you must practice accountability. You can claim to value feedback, but if you never hold people accountable to your expectations, they will walk all over you. Accountability is what produces change and brings the most benefit to the organization and the individual.

Let's go back to the question you answered at the beginning of this book. Who is in your leadership hall of fame? Who has impacted your life because of their willingness to give you the feedback you needed to hear?

Some of you can look back and identify the English teacher who nurtured your talent for writing and didn't let you settle for good enough. Others of you can point to a coach who pushed you past your breaking point and taught you that you were capable of more than you thought you could accomplish. Today, you still hear their voice in your head encouraging you when you want to give up. And some of you are imagining a mentor or pastor, someone who listened to you, heard you out, and challenged you to be better. They answered your hard questions but weren't afraid to ask you even harder ones. What feedback did they give you? How did they get to know you better? What showed you that they truly cared?

Whoever you're thinking of, your life would not be the same if they hadn't set expectations, given you feedback, and held you accountable. Your individual drive can get you only so far. Everyone needs someone who can provide external motivation.

I don't know about you, but I'm not going to let my mentors' legacy stop with me. I'm determined to be in other people's leadership hall of fame. I want people to

BUILDING YOUR LEADERSHIP LEGACY

look back on their lives and say that my care, support, and feedback allowed them to change their lives for the better and achieve their biggest goals.

So, whose leadership hall of fame will you be in? Your feedback could be the very thing that helps them reach their goals or encourages them to keep after their dreams. There is someone in your life who needs you to believe in them enough to overcome your discomfort and give them feedback. They need someone who knows that feedback is the key to growth.

I have never regretted giving someone the feedback they needed to hear. The more I give feedback, the more I see people reach their goals and change their lives. That does not mean it's easy, even for me. You have to be willing to have tough conversations and invest significant time into people. But giving feedback is always worth it. I truly believe that if you embrace the principles of feedback and apply them to your team, you will change lives and culture for the better.

Reflection Questions

How have your thoughts on giving feedback changed since you started reading this book? What shift was the most powerful for you? What will the biggest change be when you start giving meaningful feedback?

Application Activity

Think back through the material in this book. What mindset toward feedback has prevented you from giving meaningful feedback to your employees? What technique do you want to start using right away? Work with your boss, a mentor, or a peer to set goals for how you will start implementing the techniques in this book. Encourage them to hold you accountable. Schedule a weekly check-in to talk about how you made deposits, gave redirecting and reinforcing feedback, and held people accountable.

ACKNOWLEDGMENTS

No one achieves success alone, and this book is no exception. It is the culmination of countless conversations, moments of inspiration, and the steadfast support of those who have walked alongside me on this journey. To the mentors who sparked my passion for leadership; the friends, family, colleagues who challenged my thinking; and the team who helped bring this vision to life—thank you. This book would not exist without your wisdom, encouragement, and belief in its message.

To my writer, Abigail Condon, your talent, insight, and dedication have been invaluable to this project. Your ability to bring my thoughts to life with clarity and precision has made this book a reality. Thank you for helping shape these ideas into a resource that I hope will inspire and guide leaders for years to come. Your partnership has been a true gift. You have believed in me and my mission to serve others from the very beginning, and I am deeply grateful.

To Matt Litton, your expertise helped transform ideas into a cohesive vision, ensuring this book's

ACKNOWLEDGMENTS

structure was clear and impactful. Your ability to guide the process and ensure each piece was where it needed to be made all the difference.

To Mark Cole, Tim Elmore, and Sangram Vajre, thank you for believing in me. Your mentorship and encouragement have been inspirational throughout this process.

To my dear friend and pastor, Nathan Miller, your encouragement has been a cornerstone of my journey. You have a unique gift for calling out greatness in others. Your reminder that all things are possible through Christ, who strengthens us, has been a guiding light, especially in moments when my confidence wavered. Thank you for helping me stay rooted in faith and for being a constant source of inspiration and support.

To my clients, thank you for the privilege of working alongside you on your leadership journey. It has been an honor to support your growth and the development of your teams. Your trust, commitment, and passion for leading others have been a constant source of inspiration, and I am deeply grateful for the opportunity to be part of your story.

Lastly, to every leader I have ever had, thank you for your guidance, wisdom, and influence. Each of you has played a role in shaping the leader I am today. Your examples, lessons, and encouragement have left a lasting impact, and this book is a testament to the foundation you helped build.

NOTES

1. Paul Green, Francesca Gino, and Bradley R. Staats, "Shopping for Confirmation: How Disconfirming Feedback Shapes Social Networks," *Harvard Business Review*, September 20, 2017, https://papers.ssrn.com/sol3/papers.cfm?abstract_id=3040066.

2. Lou Solomon, "Two-Thirds of Managers Are Uncomfortable Communicating with Employees," *Harvard Business Review*, March 9, 2016, https://hbr.org/2016/03/two-thirds-of-managers-are-uncomfortable-communicating-with-employees.

3. "State of the Global Workplace: 2023 Report," Gallup, June 18, 2023, https://www.gallup.com/workplace/506879/state-global-workplace-2023-report.aspx.

4. Cheyna Brower and Nate Dvorak, "Why Employees Are Fed Up with Feedback," Gallup, October 11, 2019, https://www.gallup.com/workplace/267251/why-employees-fed-feedback.aspx#:~:text=That's%20probably%20because%2C%20as%20Gallup,at%20giving%20feedback%20to%20others.

NOTES

5. Adam Hickman, "What 'Meaningful Feedback' Means to Millennials," Gallup, January 29, 2020, https://www.gallup.com/workplace/284081/meaningful-feedback-means-millennials.aspx.

6. Chip Martin, "Brother Matthias: Martin Leo Boutlier," Society for American Baseball Research, February 10, 2020, https://sabr.org/bioproj/person/brother-matthias-martin-leo-boutlier/.

7. Martin, "Brother Matthias."

8. Matt Zajechowski, "The Worst Passive-Aggressive Phrases, According to Americans," Preply, October 22, 2024, https://preply.com/en/blog/most-passive-aggressive-phrases/.

9. Ben Wigert and Corey Tatel, "The Great Detachment: Why Employees Feel Stuck," Gallup, December 3, 2024, https://www.gallup.com/workplace/653711/great-detachment-why-employees-feel-stuck.aspx.

10. Ben Wigert and Jim Harter, "Re-Engineering Performance Management," Gallup, 2017, https://www.gallup.com/workplace/238064/re-engineering-performance-management.aspx?thank-you-report-form=1.

11. Gary Drevitch, "The Gottman Ratio for Happy Relationships at Work," *Psychology Today*, June 29, 2022, https://www.psychologytoday.com/us/blog/curating-your-life/202206/the-gottman-ratio-happy-relationships-work.

12. Ibraheem Rehman et al., "Classical Conditioning," in *StatPearls*, StatPearls Publishing, September 5, 2024, https://www.ncbi.nlm.nih.gov/books/NBK470326/.

NOTES

13. Jack Zenger and Joseph Folkman, "Why Do So Many Managers Avoid Giving Praise?," *Harvard Business Review*, May 2, 2017, https://hbr.org/2017/05/why-do-so -many-managers-avoid-giving-praise.

14. Solomon, "Two-Thirds of Managers."

15. Corinne Post et al., "Participative or Directive Leadership Behaviors for Decision-Making in Crisis Management Teams?," *Small Group Research* 53, no. 5 (2022): 692–724, https://doi.org/10.1177/10464964221087952.

16. Jodi Schulz, "Eye Contact: Don't Make These Mistakes," Michigan State University Extension, December 31, 2012, https://www.canr.msu.edu/news/eye_contact _dont_make_these_mistakes.

17. Ken Blanchard and Spencer Johnson, *The One Minute Manager* (William Morrow & Co., 1982).

18. "How Past Feedback Fuels Performance," Gallup, November 22, 2022, https://www.corporatelearning network.com/leadership/articles/how-fast-feedback-fuels -performance.

Ready to level up your leadership?
Scan the QR code and grab your free bonus resources!

You'll receive access to an exclusive interview with Jeff Hancher and our Leadership Toolkit, a comprehensive collection of our best resources for building relationships, setting expectations, building strong leadership habits, and finding a mentor.